STEPHEN FORD

COLIN WOFFIND

THE GUINNESS BOOK OF

SKILFUL
Soccer

GUINNESS PUBLISHING

THE AUTHORS

Stephen Ford is the Football Development Officer at
Brighton and Hove Albion, and is a qualified FA Coach.
He has played at professional level.

Colin Woffinden has worked for the past eight years
helping to develop the young players at Brighton and Hove
Albion. As a player he was involved with England at amateur
level and played professionally for Brighton.

Editor: Charles Richards
Text design and layout: Kathy Aldridge
Cover design: Ad Vantage Studios

Published in Great Britain by Guinness Publishing Ltd,
33 London Road, Enfield, Middlesex

Typeset in Plantin and Gill by Ace Filmsetting Ltd,
Frome, Somerset

Printed and bound in Great Britain by
The Bath Press, Bath, Avon

'Guinness' is a registered trademark of
Guinness Publishing Ltd

British Library Cataloguing in Publication Data
Woffinden, Colin
Skilful soccer
1. Association football. Techniques
I. Title   II. Ford, Stephen
796.3342

ISBN 0-85112-969-2

Contents

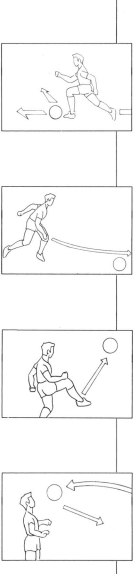

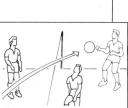

Introduction

The best players in the world today and the great players of the past have one thing in common – GREAT INDIVIDUAL BALL SKILLS.

Although they were born with talent, their skill was developed with hours and hours of practice. They would play with anything that rolled, wherever they could, by themselves or with friends. Through the sheer joy of playing and practising with a ball, they became masters of it.

This book contains over 150 different ideas and practices to improve ball skills. These skillls can be practised anywhere – the back garden, street, drive or park – with any type or size of ball. As there are lots of opportunities for players to practise when they are on their own, over a third of this book is devoted to ideas which enable them to spend this time enjoyably and successfully. These individual practices are easily understood, and boys and girls as young as eight will be able to pick out a skill they wish to practise themselves. A wall chart, enabling young players to plot their own progress, is a good idea.

The rest of the practices involve pairs and small groups. In the pair practices, one of the pair need not always be a practising player. Mum, Dad or a friend could act as a server or scorer and help with the key coaching points. All of the practices involve the use of a ball and are divided into five sections: WARM-UPS, PASSING, SHOOTING, HEADING and SMALL-SIDED GAMES.

Each section starts with a brief introduction and key coaching points. These will provide ideas as to the techniques involved. They are not hard and fast rules, as each individual will find his or her own style and method which suits them best. The coaching points are all followed by Individual Practices, then Pair Practices, and finally Group Practices. The Small-Sided Games section, starting with an introduction and ten key points for coaches, consists simply of games for groups of players. All of the practices described are accompanied by explanatory diagrams. When a playing area is required, the size can be adjusted to suit the age and amount of players in the group. If an area needs to be marked out – although markers are best – anything will do.

Variations accompany every practice, and in some cases they are practices in their own right, so there is no need to use all of them in one session. The Helpful Hints ensure that the practices are enjoyable and successful.

TIPS FOR USING THIS BOOK

Use the description of each practice and its illustration TOGETHER – remember, the illustration may not always show the size of the playing area needed for Group Practices or the distance between you and a partner for Pair Practices – but everything you need to know about each practice will be in its accompanying description.

Different types of arrow have been used to show movement of the ball and movements of the player, as follows:

⟹ movement of the ball

▫▫▫▷ movement of player

1

WARM UPS

WARM-UPS

The following warm-ups involve important skills in their own right – there is a lot of activity and plenty of touches with the ball. Players will be practising controlling, dribbling and running with the ball.

The Individual Practices can be done in whatever space is available – players simply need a ball. All of these practices are easily understood and will help to improve a wide variety of skills whilst at the same time being fun.

Younger players should always try to keep a count of their successful attempts – for example, how many times out of ten can they trap the ball without losing control? (With a wall chart they can check their progress over a period of weeks.) Running with the ball, and dribbling, can be timed over a set distance.

The Pair Practices involve either one serving while the other works, or two players competing against each other. They add a little more competition with players attempting to become more successful and skilful than each other.

The Group Practices allow players to use their individual skills within a team situation, or competing individually against each other.

KEY COACHING POINTS FOR WARM-UP PRACTICES

CONTROL

Whether the foot, thigh or chest is used, the basic technique for control is always the same. It is to withdraw that part of the body which is being used for control at the moment contact is made with the ball. The one exception is when the ball is trapped between the underside of the foot and the ground. Most importantly, in order to be more successful, players must adjust their position moving into the line of the oncoming ball.

CONTROL USING THE UNDERSIDE OF THE FOOT – THE TRAP

The trap is the easiest way of controlling the ball with the foot. When executed correctly it stops immediately under the player's foot, allowing the player complete control of the ball.

CONTROL USING THE TOP OF THE FOOT

This controlling action allows players to control the ball, yet keep it a few centimetres out in front of them. This is the most common form of control with the foot, when a high ball is arriving towards, and at the feet of, the player about to control.

CONTROL USING THE INSIDE OF THE FOOT

This controlling action allows players to quickly control the ball out in front of them and at the same time place the ball in a good position ready for them to pass, run with the ball, dribble or shoot.

CONTROL USING THE THIGH

This action is used when the ball arrives at a height between the chest and the foot. It allows players to set the ball down on the ground just in front of them. Again the player is ready to run with the ball, dribble or shoot.

CONTROL USING THE CHEST

This controlling action is used when the ball is arriving directly at the player between the head and the waist. When executed correctly, the ball drops to the ground just in front of the player, enabling them to pass, run with the ball, dribble or shoot.

CONTROL USING THE HEAD

This controlling action is used when the ball arrives at head height. It can be used to drop the ball down to the feet of the controlling player or to guide the ball into space in front of them.

DRIBBLING

Dribbling the ball involves keeping close control whilst trying to beat opponents. Players should

W A R M - U P S

take short steps, keeping the ball close to their feet at all times. They should keep their bodies over the ball where possible, and although watching the ball, they must try and look up to see what is in front of them.

RUNNING WITH THE BALL

This technique is a means by which players can move at speed with the ball. The speed at which they are running, and the amount of space they have to run into, will dictate the distance they can push the ball out in front of them, but the ball should not be more than two paces away.

Individual Practices

UNDERSIDE OF THE FOOT TRAP **1**

Stand 5 metres away from and facing the wall. Throw the ball against the wall, so that it comes back to your feet. Trap the ball between the sole of your foot and the ground.

TOP OF THE FOOT TRAP **2**

Stand 5 metres away from and facing the wall. Throw the ball against the wall, and control it, with the top of your foot, bringing it down to the ground at your feet.

SIDE OF THE FOOT TRAP **3**

Stand 5 metres away from and facing the wall. Throw the ball against the wall. As it returns, control the ball with the side of your foot, bringing it slightly out in front of you.

V A R I A T I O N S

- Increase and decrease the distance you stand from the wall.

- Try the practices with a smaller ball.

- Throw the ball against the wall, turn completely around, and control the ball.

- The ball can be thrown lower against the wall, making you move forward to control the ball.

- Throw the ball harder against the wall, making you take a few steps backwards to control the ball.

W A R M - U P S

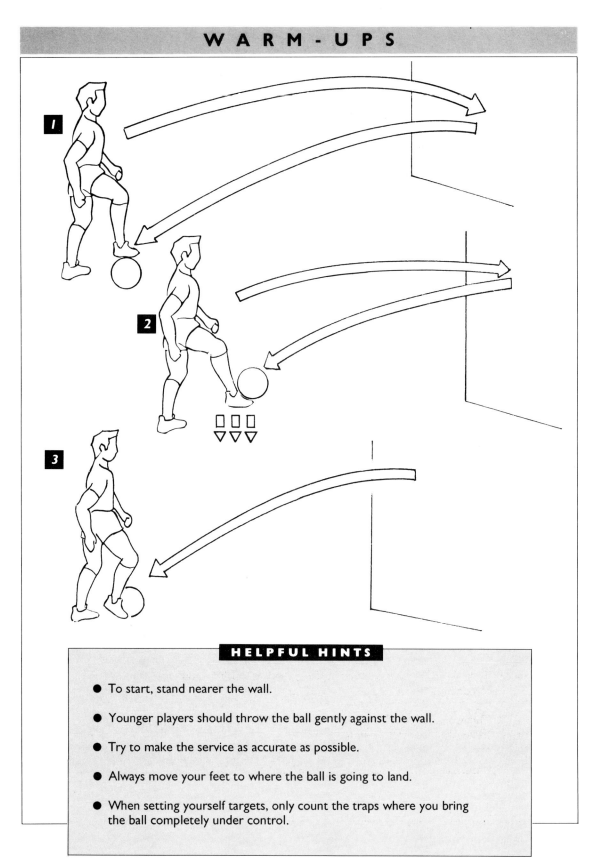

HELPFUL HINTS

- To start, stand nearer the wall.

- Younger players should throw the ball gently against the wall.

- Try to make the service as accurate as possible.

- Always move your feet to where the ball is going to land.

- When setting yourself targets, only count the traps where you bring the ball completely under control.

WARM-UPS

THIGH TRAP **1**

Stand 5 metres away from and facing the wall. Throw the ball against the wall so that it returns between your head and your knee. The ball should drop gently off your thigh, and down onto the ground just in front of you.

CHEST TRAP **2**

Stand 5 metres away from and facing the wall. Throw the ball gently against the wall, so that it returns between your head and your waist. The ball should drop off your chest and down to your feet.

HEAD TRAP **3**

Stand 5 metres away from and facing the wall. Throw the ball gently against the wall, so that it returns to you at head height. The controlling header should set the ball down in front of you. This is the most difficult controlling skill.

VARIATIONS

- Control the ball on either thigh.
- Try to control the ball from your chest, onto your thigh, and then to the ground.
- Increase and decrease the distance you stand from the wall.
- Try to first control the ball, and then with the use of the thigh, head and chest, keep it in the air for five touches, before dropping it to the ground at your feet.
- Throw the ball high against the wall, letting it bounce once, before using your thigh, head or chest to control the ball.

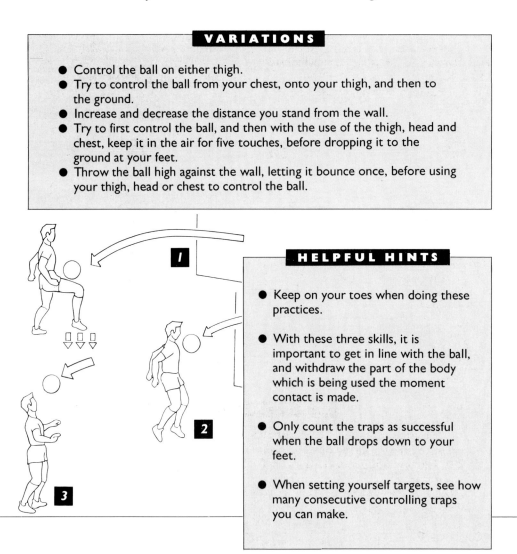

HELPFUL HINTS

- Keep on your toes when doing these practices.

- With these three skills, it is important to get in line with the ball, and withdraw the part of the body which is being used the moment contact is made.

- Only count the traps as successful when the ball drops down to your feet.

- When setting yourself targets, see how many consecutive controlling traps you can make.

W A R M - U P S

FOOT CONTROL **1**

Throw the ball 5 metres into the air above your head. Adjust your position, allowing you to trap the ball between the sole of your foot and the ground.

TOP OF THE FOOT CONTROL **2**

Throw the ball 5 metres into the air above your head, adjust your position, and with the use of the top part of your foot, control the ball just above the ground, letting it roll gently out in front of you.

THIGH CONTROL **3**

Throw the ball 5 metres into the air above your head. Adjust your position, and with the use of your thigh, control the ball and let it drop gently to the ground.

V A R I A T I O N S

- Use your weaker foot.
- Vary the height of your service.
- Throw the ball slightly up and out in front of you.
- Throw the ball up just behind you.
- Run and throw the ball into the air, then control it using any of the above controlling skills.

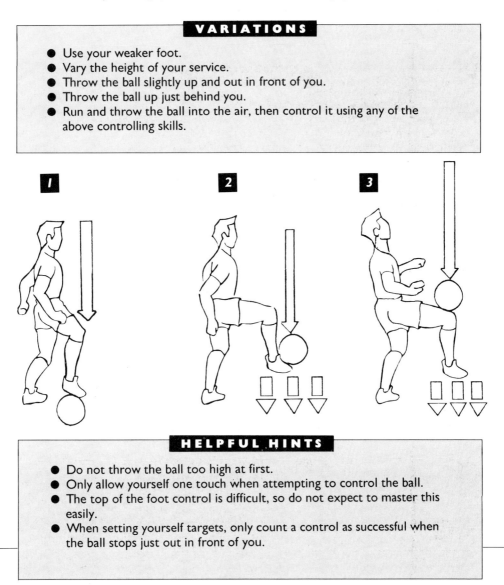

H E L P F U L H I N T S

- Do not throw the ball too high at first.
- Only allow yourself one touch when attempting to control the ball.
- The top of the foot control is difficult, so do not expect to master this easily.
- When setting yourself targets, only count a control as successful when the ball stops just out in front of you.

W A R M - U P S

CONTROL MOVING FORWARDS **1**

Start with the ball at your feet. Using alternate feet, and by touching the top of the ball with the sole of your foot, move forwards with the ball.

CONTROL MOVING BACKWARDS **2**

Start with the ball at your feet. Using alternate feet, and by touching the top of the ball with the sole of your foot, move backwards with the ball.

CONTROL CHANGING DIRECTION **3**

Start with the ball at your feet. Using alternate feet, roll the sole of your foot over the top of the ball, moving it to the left and to the right.

V A R I A T I O N S

- Without moving and by alternately using the sole of your left and right foot, touch the top of the ball, as quickly as possible.
- Try these practices without looking at the ball.
- By bringing your foot down the side of the ball, try to get it to roll over your foot.
- Practise these skills while moving around markers.
- Combine the three controlling practices.

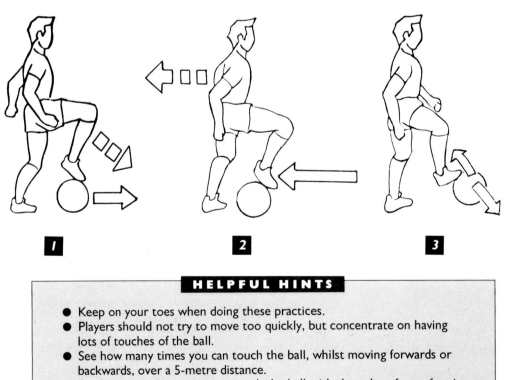

1　　　　　　　**2**　　　　　　　**3**

H E L P F U L   H I N T S

- Keep on your toes when doing these practices.
- Players should not try to move too quickly, but concentrate on having lots of touches of the ball.
- See how many times you can touch the ball, whilst moving forwards or backwards, over a 5-metre distance.
- See how many times you can touch the ball with the soles of your feet in a minute.

W A R M - U P S

BASIC DRIBBLING █1

Keeping the ball just out in front of you, and by touching it with alternate feet, move slowly around a small area, changing your direction after every three or four touches.

DRIBBLING AT SPEED █2

Keeping the ball just out in front of you, try to move as quickly as possible while keeping close control of the ball.

CONTROLLED DRIBBLING █3

Set out six markers, each 1 metre apart. Dribble in and out of these markers, rounding the end one, before dribbling in and out back to the start.

VARIATIONS

● Decrease the distance between each marker.

● Dribble in and out of the markers, only using the outside of each foot.

● Dribble in and out of the markers, only using the inside of each foot.

● Dribble completely around each marker, before moving to the next.

● Dribble backwards around the markers.

HELPFUL HINTS

● When first practising these skills, try them at walking pace.

● When control becomes easier, practise looking up while still moving and controlling the ball.

● Never rush the control, master this before you introduce speed or markers.

● Set yourself targets by dribbling in and out of six markers in a set time. Try to improve on your best time.

W A R M - U P S

START-STOP DRIBBLE **1**

Stand with the ball at your feet. Dribble the ball forward at pace. Quickly put your foot on the top of the ball, stopping it (and yourself) completely still. Dribble forwards again, and continue the practice.

DRAG-BACK AND DRIBBLE **2**

Stand with the ball at your feet. Dribble the ball forward at pace. Quickly put your foot on top of the ball, dragging it back towards you. With the use of either foot, move the ball forward and continue with the dribble.

DRAG-BACK, CHANGE DIRECTION AND DRIBBLE **3**

Stand with the ball at your feet. Dribble the ball forward at pace. Quickly put your foot on the top of the ball, dragging it back behind your other foot and to the side of you. Without stopping, continue dribbling in the new direction with the ball. Repeat the practice, continually changing direction.

V A R I A T I O N S

- Try these practices dribbling as fast as you can.

- When attempting the start–stop dribble, after stopping, move off in the opposite direction.

- Practice feinting to drag the ball back, but without making contact with the ball, continue the dribble.

- Try combining these practices – follow the start–stop with the drag-back and then the change of direction skill.

H E L P F U L   H I N T S

- Take short steps, and use both feet when dribbling the ball.

- Young players should start by practising drag-backs slowly.

- Although it's important to concentrate on the ball, look up whenever possible.

- Your body should be completely over the ball when doing these practices.

- Following the drag-backs, players must turn as quickly as possible to stay in control of the ball.

W A R M - U P S

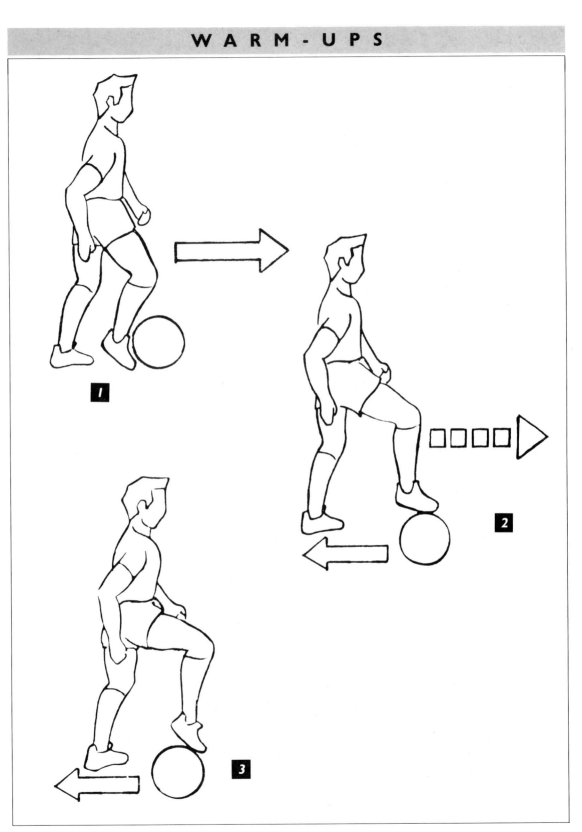

WARM-UPS

BASIC RUNNING WITH THE BALL   **1**

Start with the ball at your feet. Play the ball forward 2 metres, run after it, and keep it moving forward with the use of the outside of the foot of your leading leg.

RUNNING WITH THE BALL AT SPEED   **2**

Starting with the ball at your feet, try to run as fast as you can, whilst keeping the ball no more than two paces out in front of you.

RUNNING AND TURNING   **3**

Place a marker 20 metres away from you. Moving with the ball as fast as you can, but keeping it under control, run to the marker and back. Add two more markers to form a square, and practise running and turning with the ball, around the outside of the square.

VARIATIONS

- Practise running with the ball and suddenly changing speed to go faster.
- Run with the ball, change direction, and move as quickly as possible over the next 5 metres.
- Run both to the right and left around the square.
- Try practising lots of standing starts. Run with the ball for 10 metres, then stop and do the practice again.

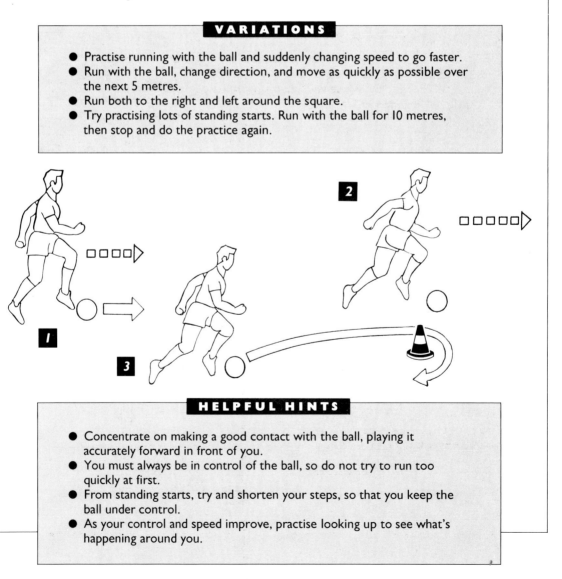

HELPFUL HINTS

- Concentrate on making a good contact with the ball, playing it accurately forward in front of you.
- You must always be in control of the ball, so do not try to run too quickly at first.
- From standing starts, try and shorten your steps, so that you keep the ball under control.
- As your control and speed improve, practise looking up to see what's happening around you.

W A R M - U P S

TRICK ONE   **1**

Stand with the ball at your feet. Place your foot on top of the ball, and drag it back towards you. Quickly move your foot under the ball, whilst it is moving backwards, and flick it up into the air.

TRICK TWO   **2**

Stand with the ball between your feet. Simultaneously bring your toes together under the ball, and it will flick up into the air.

TRICK THREE   **3**

Stand with the ball at your feet. Strike down on the side of the ball with your foot. The ball will spin upwards into the air.

VARIATIONS

- Once the ball is in the air, see how many times you can keep the ball up, without it touching the ground.
- Try tricks one and three with your weaker foot.
- Try these tricks with a smaller ball.
- Whilst moving backwards or forwards in control of the ball, attempt trick one.

HELPFUL HINTS

- All your foot movements must be very quick.

- Remember these tricks are not easy to do – it will take you time to perfect them.

- You never need to pick the ball up with your hands – always try to use a trick to get the ball from the ground to your hands.

- Set yourself targets, trying to do five consecutive tricks. Can you do more?

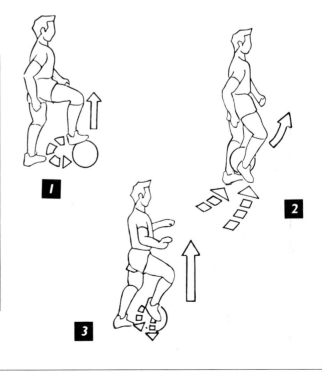

W A R M - U P S

TRICK FOUR   4

Hold the ball firmly between your ankles. As quickly as possible, bend both knees, jump and bring your ankles up behind you, releasing the ball into the air.

TRICK FIVE   5

Stand with the ball at your feet. Place one foot over the ball, back-heeling it onto the front of your standing foot. The ball will flick up into the air.

TRICK SIX   6

Stand with the ball at your feet. Place one foot directly in front of the ball, with the other behind it. Using your back foot, roll the ball up the back of your front leg. When the ball is just above your ankle, your back leg releases the ball allowing your front leg to back-heel it into the air.

VARIATIONS

- Instead of catching the ball, use your head, feet and thighs to keep it off the ground.
- When doing tricks four or six, try to get the ball to come over your head into your hands.
- Whilst moving forward dribbling the ball, try trick six.
- Use one of these tricks to get the ball into the air, and then volley it at a target.

HELPFUL HINTS

- By using a larger ball, the tricks become easier.
- Master one trick at a time.
- The idea is to get the ball into the air, so try and find your own ways to do this.
- Try to do one or more of these tricks whenever you are playing or practising.

WARM-UPS

JUGGLING THE BALL WITH YOUR FEET **1**

Drop the ball gently towards your foot. The aim is now to keep the ball up in the air, and under control, by using the top of either foot.

JUGGLING THE BALL WITH YOUR THIGH **2**

Drop the ball onto your thigh. The aim is to keep the ball up in the air, and under control, by using either thigh.

JUGGLING THE BALL WITH YOUR FEET, THIGHS, CHEST AND SHOULDERS **3**

Drop the ball gently towards your feet. Try to keep the ball up in the air, and under control, by using your foot, thigh, chest and shoulders.

VARIATIONS

- Try to balance the ball on top of your foot.
- Try to balance the ball on the back of your neck.
- By using a trick, flick the ball into the air, and juggle.
- Try to keep the ball under control by juggling it with the same foot or thigh.
- Vary the height you play the ball back into the air when using your foot or thigh.
- Try to juggle the ball in a certain order; go from your foot, to thigh, to shoulder, to chest, to thigh and foot and onto the ground to finish.

HELPFUL HINTS

- Younger players should start by dropping the ball onto their foot or thigh and controlling it just once before catching it. Gradually increase the amount of controlling touches.
- Always watch the ball carefully.
- When juggling, keep the ball as close to you as possible.
- The best scores are achieved by being able to keep the ball under control, using all parts of the body.

Pair
Practices

DRIBBLING WITH TURNS 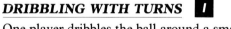 1

One player dribbles the ball around a small area, and on a call from the other player, quickly turns around and dribbles in the opposite direction. Change roles after one minute and continue the practice.

DRIBBLING WITH TRICKS 2

One player dribbles the ball around a small area, and on a call from the other player, has to perform a certain skill. 'TRICK' – pretend to beat an opponent; 'CHANGE' – dribble off in a new direction; or 'SHARP' – dribble quickly forward for three or four paces. Each player works for 2 minutes and then they change roles.

VARIATIONS

DRIBBLING WITH TURNS
● All the turns must be done with a drag-back.
● Use the weaker foot to do the turns.
● Try to turn and dribble more quickly.

DRIBBLING WITH TRICKS
● Dribble using only the inside or only the outside of your foot.
● Dribble the ball with alternate feet, either by touching the top of the ball or rolling your foot over the top of it.
● Add 'STOP' to the instructions called out, to see if the working player is in control of the ball.

W A R M - U P S

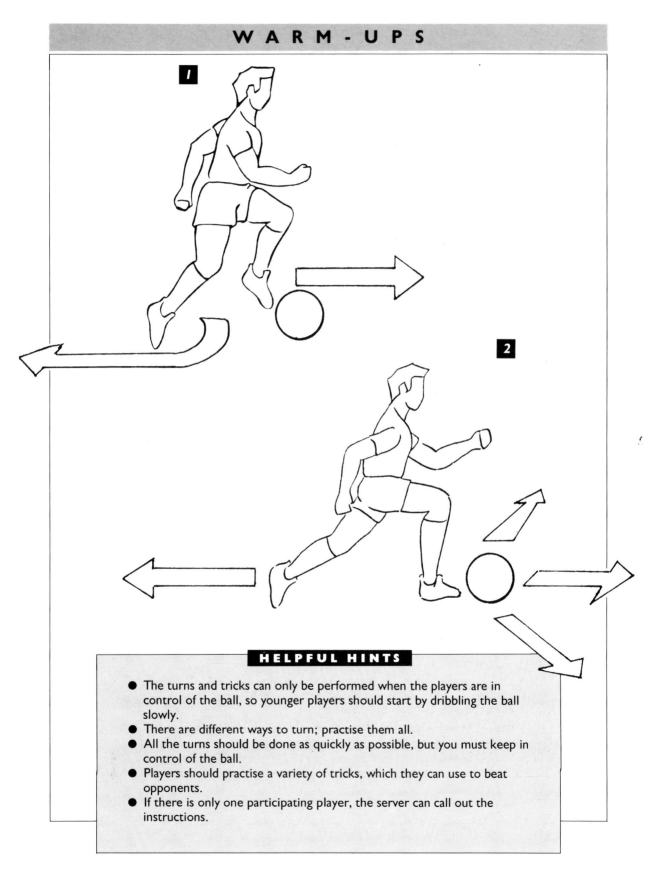

1

2

- The turns and tricks can only be performed when the players are in control of the ball, so younger players should start by dribbling the ball slowly.
- There are different ways to turn; practise them all.
- All the turns should be done as quickly as possible, but you must keep in control of the ball.
- Players should practise a variety of tricks, which they can use to beat opponents.
- If there is only one participating player, the server can call out the instructions.

W A R M - U P S

REACTION DRIBBLING **1**

One player has the ball, and stands 1 metre away from and facing a partner. The object of the practice is for the player with the ball to dribble to either of the two markers, placed 5 metres away on either side. Once the ball has been played, the opposing player tries to prevent the dribbling player from reaching the markers. The practice continues with the players changing roles.

POSSESSION DRIBBLING **2**

Within a small area, the object of the game is for the player who starts with the ball to keep it away from the other. When the defending player wins the ball, the roles are reversed.

VARIATIONS

REACTION DRIBBLING
- Increase or decrease the distance the markers are placed from the players.
- Allow the defending player to start the practice by calling 'GO'.

POSSESSION DRIBBLING
- The defending player can only make a tackle when face to face with the player who has the ball.
- Ask the player with the ball to keep possession but do not allow them to move around the area with it.

HELPFUL HINTS

- When practising possession dribbling, players should try to keep their bodies between the defender and the ball.

- In reaction dribbling, encourage players to feint – to go in one direction before playing the ball in the other.

- Make possession dribbling more competitive by seeing which player retains possession the longest.

- Reaction dribbling can be made more competitive by seeing which player reaches a marker most times from 10 attempts.

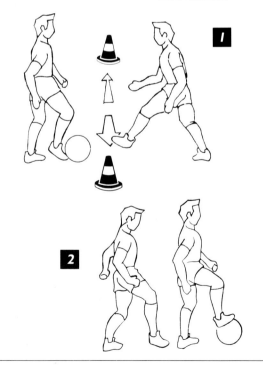

W A R M - U P S

QUICK CONTROL **1**

Two players stand 5 metres apart, facing each other. The player with the ball throws it to a partner who controls and traps the ball as quickly as possible under the sole of the foot. The controlling player picks up the ball and throws it back for the first player to control. The practice continues.

REACT AND CONTROL **2**

The two players stand 5 metres apart. One player has the ball and acts as a server, and the other player, who is facing away from the server, is the working player. The server throws the ball calling 'TURN' to the working player who turns, controls the ball and passes it back to the server. The practice continues, with the players changing roles after a set period of time or number of turns.

V A R I A T I O N S

QUICK CONTROL
- Vary the service and allow the players to use any part of the body to control the ball.
- Try this practice with one player receiving 10 consecutive serves.

REACT AND CONTROL
- Ask the receiving player to start by sitting down facing in the opposite direction.
- The player controlling the ball is only allowed two touches, one to control, the other to make the returning pass.
- Vary the height and speed of the service.
- Ask the receiving player to turn both to the right and to the left.

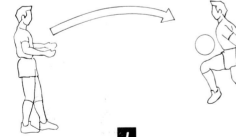

1

2

H E L P F U L   H I N T S

- Younger players should throw the ball gently at first.
- Only when the ball is stationary under a player's foot is the control successful.
- As the players improve, shorten the servicing distance.
- Add a competitive edge, with each player counting how many consecutive successful controls they can make.

WARM-UPS

CONTROL AND PASS **1**

Stand 10 metres away from and facing your partner. The server throws the ball to the feet of the working player, who controls the ball with the sole of the foot, and passes it back to the server. After practising this, move onto control with the top and side of the foot. To practise the thigh, chest and head control, the server throws the ball between the head and the knee of the working player. After a period of time the players change roles.

CONTROL, DRIBBLE AND PASS **2**

Stand 5 metres away from and facing your partner. Place a marker 5 metres behind the working player. The server throws the ball to the receiving player who controls it, turns and dribbles around the marker, before passing it back to the server. Vary the height of the service to practise the thigh, chest and head controlling actions.

VARIATIONS

CONTROL AND PASS
- Try this practice with a smaller ball.
- The server, just before serving the ball, calls out the part of the body to be used to control the ball.
- Stand facing away from the server, and only turn around when the server shouts 'GO'.

CONTROL, DRIBBLE AND PASS
- Ask the receiving player to control the ball, dribble around the server and return to the starting point, before returning the pass.
- As soon as the receiving player has touched the ball, the server tries to get to the marker first.

1

2

HELPFUL HINTS

- Younger players should serve the ball gently at first.
- All of the controlling practices are fun, but the foot trap is the most important. Spend as much time as you can on this.
- Players should practise turning both ways.
- To add a competitive element, or to set a target to improve upon, ask the server to keep a score of your successful attempts.

W A R M - U P S

DRIBBLING TO SCORE 1

One player stands with the ball on a line. The other player stands on a line opposite, 10 metres away. The player in possession dribbles the ball forward with the aim of stopping it on their opponent's line. The opposing player must defend their line. If the attacking player is successful, the possession goes to the defender, who in turn tries to reach their opponent's line. The practice continues with the player in possession attacking the line opposite.

DRIBBLING RACE 2

Both players stand on the same line, each with a ball at their feet. On a signal, both players attempt to dribble the ball over an agreed line, or point opposite, before turning and dribbling back to the starting line. The first player back wins. The practice continues with the losing player giving the signal for the next race to start.

VARIATIONS

DRIBBLING TO SCORE
- The defender can only move along their own goal line when trying to prevent the other player scoring.
- The defending player starts the practice by passing the ball to the attacker, who controls and dribbles forward.
- Mark out two 1-metre wide goals on the goal lines and try to dribble through your opponent's goal.

DRIBBLING RACE
- Try lengthening the race – go to the agreed point and back five times.
- Face the opposite way, and on a signal, turn and dribble to the line and back.
- Start by sitting on the ground, quickly get up and dribble to the line and back.
- Dribble out forward to the line and backward to the start.

HELPFUL HINTS

- Younger players can start the dribble-to-score practice by just running the ball over the line to score.

- Do not race over more than 10 metres.

- Agree on the width of the area you are playing in and if the attacking player goes out of this area, the possession is lost.

- When dribbling to score, use the tricks you have practised to beat the defending player.

- Make the dribbling-to-score practice into a competitive game by seeing who scores 10 goals first.

WARM-UPS

JUGGLING IN PAIRS **1**

The two players stand facing each other 2 metres apart. One player, holding the ball, gently throws it to the other. This player, without the use of hands, controls it, keeping it off the ground, and with the second touch returns the ball to their partner who likewise controls it with one touch, and returns it with the next. The practice continues with the two players trying to keep the ball in the air for as long as possible.

FOOTBALL TENNIS **2**

Mark out two areas of 3 metres square with a gap of 3 metres between them. Each player stands in a square. The game is started with one player, from the back of their square, side-footing the ball so that it lands in their opponent's square. This player, taking no more than two touches, must return the ball, so that it bounces in their opponent's square. The game continues until one of the players miscontrols the ball or their pass fails to land in their opponent's square. Each player is allowed to let the ball hit the ground, in their area, once each time. Each player takes it in turn to serve the ball.

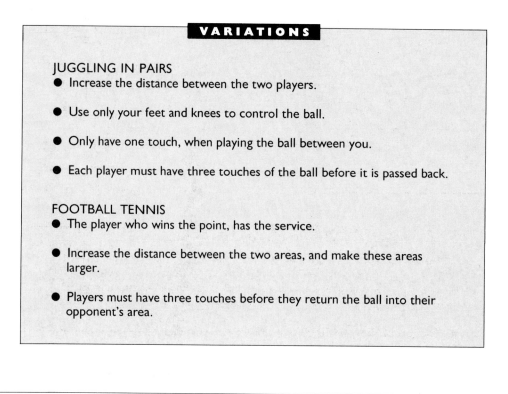

VARIATIONS

JUGGLING IN PAIRS
- Increase the distance between the two players.

- Use only your feet and knees to control the ball.

- Only have one touch, when playing the ball between you.

- Each player must have three touches of the ball before it is passed back.

FOOTBALL TENNIS
- The player who wins the point, has the service.

- Increase the distance between the two areas, and make these areas larger.

- Players must have three touches before they return the ball into their opponent's area.

WARM-UPS

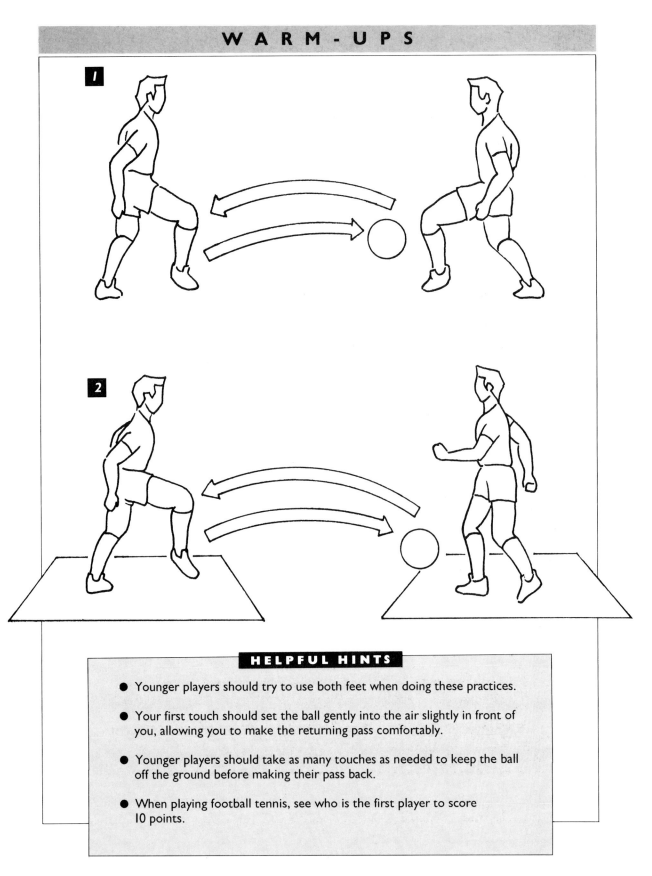

HELPFUL HINTS

● Younger players should try to use both feet when doing these practices.

● Your first touch should set the ball gently into the air slightly in front of you, allowing you to make the returning pass comfortably.

● Younger players should take as many touches as needed to keep the ball off the ground before making their pass back.

● When playing football tennis, see who is the first player to score 10 points.

Group Practices

WARM-UPS

NUMBER OF PLAYERS

5 or more.

EQUIPMENT

A ball for each group.

PLAYING AREA

10 metres by 10 metres.

THE PRACTICE

The group of players, with one ball between them, form a circle. The object of this practice is for the group of players to keep the ball off the ground without using their hands. The practice starts with one player gently throwing the ball to another in the circle. The receiving player, without taking more than two touches, passes the ball through the air to another player. The practice continues with the ball being moved around the circle. When the ball touches the ground it is picked up and the practice is re-started.

VARIATIONS

● Ask the players to have only one touch.

● Decrease and increase the size of the circle.

● Make each player have at least three touches before passing the ball on.

● Don't allow the receiving player to pass the ball directly back to the player who has just passed the ball.

● Give each player a number and pass the ball in turn – 1 to 2; 2 to 3; 3 to 4 and so on.

● Allow the players to use only their feet to control the ball and pass it on.

● Place one player in the middle and make every other pass go to that player.

W A R M - U P S

HELPFUL HINTS

● Ensure all the players are on their toes ready to move to receive the ball.

● With younger players, allow the ball to touch the ground once, encouraging them to keep the practice going.

● Don't have too many players in one group – split large numbers of players into two or three groups.

● Make this practice competitive by seeing if the circle of players can keep the ball in the air for one minute.

● If you have two or more groups, see which is the first group to 'drop' the ball.

W A R M - U P S

NUMBER OF PLAYERS

3 or more.

EQUIPMENT

A ball for each player, and markers.

PLAYING AREA

10 metres by 10 metres.

THE PRACTICE

The players have a ball each and stand inside the area. The object of the practice is for each player to dribble their ball around inside the playing area, but at the same time trying to kick any of the others out of the square. Players must be in control of their own ball before trying to kick somebody else's ball out. Each player starts with 10 points and loses 1 point every time their ball goes out of the square. The player with the most points at the end of the game is the winner. The end of the game can either be when one player loses all of their points or after a certain period of time.

VARIATIONS

- Ask the players to keep on the move and deduct a point if you see them stop.
- Ask the players to move around backwards whilst controlling the ball.
- Ask the players to use only their right foot when dribbling.
- Ask the players to use only their left foot when dribbling.
- Decrease and increase the size of the area.
- If a player's ball goes out of the square, this player cannot return. The last player left in the area is the winner.

HELPFUL HINTS

- Stop the practice at various intervals to introduce the variations and to keep a check on players' scores.

- If soccer balls are not available you can still play this game by using any size or type of ball.

- Position two markers, 3 metres apart, on one edge of the playing area and make all players return through these markers to get back into the playing area.

- If you do not have enough soccer balls for every player, form pairs and apply the same rules.

W A R M - U P S

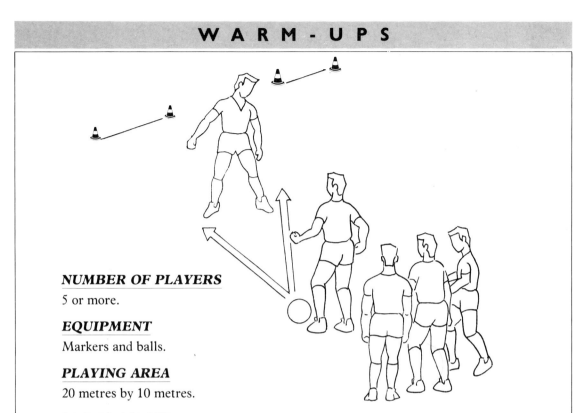

NUMBER OF PLAYERS

5 or more.

EQUIPMENT

Markers and balls.

PLAYING AREA

20 metres by 10 metres.

THE PRACTICE

On a line mark out two goals, 1 metre wide and 10 metres apart. One defending player starts 5 metres in front of and between the two goals. The object of this practice is for each attacking player in turn, starting 15 metres from the goals, to dribble past the defender and score in either of the goals. After a set period of time, one of the attacking players changes roles with the defending player and the practice continues.

VARIATIONS

- Decrease the size of the goals.
- Bring the goals closer together.
- Allow the attacking players to score by passing the ball past the defender.
- In order to score a goal, the attackers have to stop the ball on either of the goal lines.
- Allow defenders to act as goalkeepers.

HELPFUL HINTS

- Make sure the defender is in position before the next attacker starts.
- Practise different tricks when trying to beat the defender.
- To make this practice more competitive, see how many times a defender can stop the attackers from 20 attempts.
- See which player manages to score the most goals during the practice session.
- If you have a large number of players, add another goal, another defender and have two lines of attacking players.

WARM-UPS

NUMBER OF PLAYERS

8 or more.

EQUIPMENT

A ball for each group.

PLAYING AREA

20 metres by 10 metres.

THE PRACTICE

Divide the players into teams of equal numbers. The player at the front of each team has a ball. The object of this relay practice is for each player in the team to dribble the ball to a marker 10 metres away. They dribble around the marker and back to the rear of their team. Once there they pass the ball through the legs of the team to start the next player off. The relay is completed when everybody in the team has had a turn.

VARIATIONS

- The first player dribbles out to the marker, turns, and passes the ball back to the next player in the team. They return the pass. The first player then dribbles back to the rear of the team and the next player goes.

- The first player dribbles out to the marker, then juggles the ball in the air for five consecutive touches before dribbling back to the rear of their team. The next player then goes.

- The first player dribbles out to the marker, turns, and makes a pass with every player in the team before dribbling back to the rear of their team. The next player then goes.

- The first player dribbles out to the marker and backwards to the rear of their team before the next player goes.

- The first player dribbles out to the marker, back to the rear of the team and dribbles in and out of the players in their team before the next player goes.

WARM-UPS

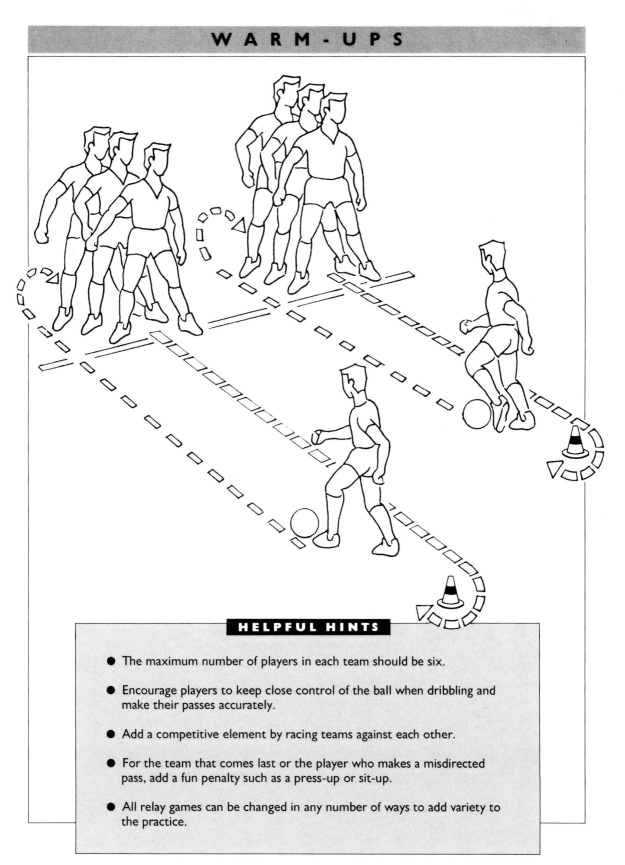

HELPFUL HINTS

● The maximum number of players in each team should be six.

● Encourage players to keep close control of the ball when dribbling and make their passes accurately.

● Add a competitive element by racing teams against each other.

● For the team that comes last or the player who makes a misdirected pass, add a fun penalty such as a press-up or sit-up.

● All relay games can be changed in any number of ways to add variety to the practice.

W A R M - U P S

NUMBER OF PLAYERS

3 or more.

EQUIPMENT

One ball for each player, and markers.

PLAYING AREA

20 metres by 10 metres.

THE PRACTICE

The players have a ball each, and stand on a line. On either side of the line, place two markers – one 5 metres away, the other 10 metres away. These are numbered 1, 2, 3 and 4. When any of these numbers are called, players dribble out, stopping the ball in line with that marker and then return to the starting line. The practice continues with the numbers being called out at random.

VARIATIONS

- Add more markers on either side of the line.
- More than one number is called out making the players dribble to each in turn.
- Change the order in which the markers are numbered.
- Ask the players to dribble to the number called out and stop there.

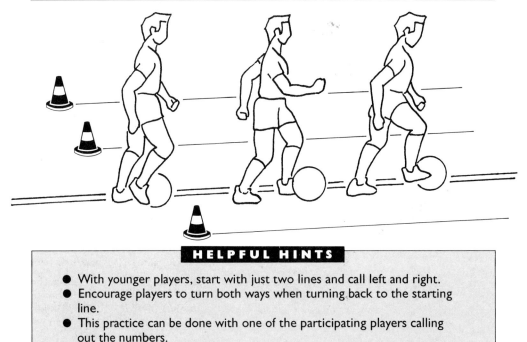

HELPFUL HINTS

- With younger players, start with just two lines and call left and right.
- Encourage players to turn both ways when turning back to the starting line.
- This practice can be done with one of the participating players calling out the numbers.
- Make this practice competitive by seeing which player returns to the starting line first ten times.
- Instead of giving the markers numbers, use names of soccer teams.

W A R M - U P S

NUMBER OF PLAYERS
8 or more.

EQUIPMENT
One ball between two players.

PLAYING AREA
20 metres by 20 metres.

THE PRACTICE
Organise the players into pairs with one ball for each pair. The pairs form a circle 20 metres across. One player from each pair gives their partner a piggy back. On a call of 'GO', the players jump off, take possession of the ball and dribble anti-clockwise around the outside of the circle before returning to the starting position. The pairs change roles and the practice continues.

VARIATIONS

- Make the players dribble clockwise around the outside of the circle.
- Make the players crawl through their partner's legs before dribbling the ball around the circle.
- On calling 'TURN', the players immediately turn and return to their partner.
- Ask the players to dribble in and out of the stationary players forming the circle.
- Ask the players to dribble completely around every player before returning.

HELPFUL HINTS

- If there are not enough players, use markers in their place.

- Make sure the stationary players do not hinder the player dribbling.

- Maintain the size of the circle required – markers can be positioned if necessary.

- To make the practice competitive, see which player is last to return to their partner after dribbling around the outside of the circle. A fun punishment, such as five sit-ups, can be given to the player who is last.

W A R M - U P S

NUMBER OF PLAYERS

5 or more.

EQUIPMENT

Markers and balls.

PLAYING AREA

20 metres by 20 metres.

THE PRACTICE

The players stand inside the playing area, with one player in possession of a ball. The object of the practice is for this player to try and tag any other player whilst dribbling the ball. When a player gets tagged, they collect another ball, joining in with the first player in trying to tag the other players. As each player gets tagged they collect a ball and the practice continues.

VARIATIONS

- Try this practice having two players with one ball, dribbling and passing it between them, trying to tag the other players.
- Allow the player in possession to pass the ball, trying to hit other players below the knees. This counts as being tagged.
- Decrease the size of the area and only allow the players dribbling to use their weaker foot.
- The tagged player takes possession of the ball and becomes the tagging player.

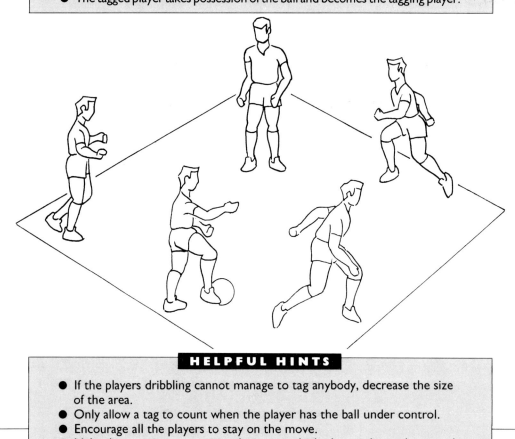

HELPFUL HINTS

- If the players dribbling cannot manage to tag anybody, decrease the size of the area.
- Only allow a tag to count when the player has the ball under control.
- Encourage all the players to stay on the move.
- Make this practice competitive, by seeing which player is last to be tagged.

PASSING

PASSING

Everything in soccer revolves around passing and controlling the ball. Each and every one of the following practices encourages the players to pass accurately. As passing looks easy, most players do not practise this skill enough. It is thought of as something everybody can do. The best players in the world, however, will practise passing for hour after hour.

The Individual Practices can quite easily be done in the back garden against the wall. Players just need a ball and a wall, and can spend as much time as they wish practising their passing skills. (With a wall chart, young players can check on their progress. For example, how many accurate passes can they make from ten attempts?)

The Pair Practices involve the use of another player or server. Again, they are easy to do and give players greater variations of practices whilst bringing in a competitive element. If one of the pair is a Mum or Dad, they can help as a server, keep a check of successful passes and guide the player using the key coaching points.

The Group Practices allow the players to use the skill of passing in a competitive situation. It helps players to understand when to pass and at what pace the pass should be made to avoid being intercepted.

Passing is something you can never practise enough, whether it's on your own, in pairs, or in a group.

KEY COACHING POINTS FOR PASSING PRACTICES

All types of passes, whether they are along the ground, high into the air, volleyed or curved, short or long, are made with the inside, outside or top of the foot. When making any of these types of passes, players should watch the ball carefully and concentrate on kicking it correctly.

LOW PASSES USING THE TOP OF THE FOOT

Strike the middle of the ball, keeping the foot firm and pointing downwards, with the body over the ball. Players should kick through the ball, as this type of pass is used over longer distances.

LOW PASSES USING THE INSIDE OF THE FOOT

Strike the middle of the ball with the side of the foot facing in the direction of the pass. Again, keep the body over the ball. Greater accuracy is achieved over short distances with these passes.

CHIPPED PASSES USING THE TOP OF THE FOOT

Strike the lower half of the ball with the foot pointing downwards. The further down the ball is kicked, the higher the ball will go. Players should dig in under the ball with the toe of their boot and stop the kicking action immediately after contact.

CURVED PASSES USING THE OUTSIDE/INSIDE OF THE FOOT

Strike the side of the ball with the outside/inside part of the foot. The ankle must be firm and there must be a full follow-through of the kicking action to achieve the curve in the pass. Keep the body over the ball.

HIGH PASSES USING THE TOP OF THE FOOT

Strike the lower half of the ball, keeping the foot firm and pointing towards the ground. Players should lean slightly back as the pass is made. Kick through the ball as this type of pass is used over long distances.

VOLLEY PASSES

Volley passes can be made with the inside, outside or top of the foot. Keep the body over the

P A S S I N G

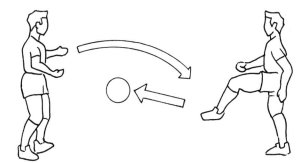

ball and the ankle firm, striking the middle of the ball as it drops towards the ground. Do not try to kick the ball too hard.

HALF-VOLLEY PASSES

These passes can be made with the inside, outside or top of the foot. Keep the body over the ball and the ankle firm, striking the middle of the ball just as it makes contact with the ground.

Individual Practices

P A S S I N G

LOW PASSES WITH THE TOP OF THE FOOT **1**

Stand 15 metres away from and facing the wall. Draw a line half a metre high across the wall. By using the top of your foot, hit the ball against the wall below the line. If your pass is good it will come straight back to you. Control the ball and repeat the practice.

LOW PASSES WITH THE SIDE OF THE FOOT **2**

Stand 15 metres away from and facing the wall. Draw a line half a metre high across the wall. By using the side of your foot, hit the ball against the wall below the line. Control the ball when it returns and repeat the practice.

HIGH PASSES WITH THE TOP OF THE FOOT **3**

Stand 15 metres away from and facing the wall. Draw a line 1 metre high across the wall. By using the top of your foot, hit the ball against the wall above the line. Control the ball when it returns and repeat the practice.

V A R I A T I O N S

- Increase the distance of the passes.

- Use both feet to make the passes.

- Play first-time passes against the wall.

- Pass the ball against the wall, control it as it returns and make the next pass with your other foot.

- Try to hit the ball as high up the wall as you can.

- Try these practices with a smaller ball.

P A S S I N G

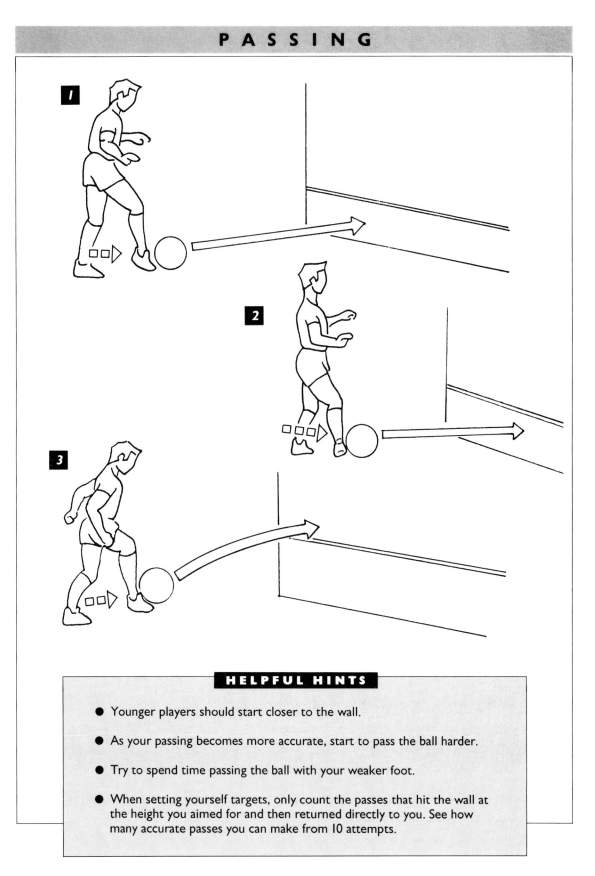

1

2

3

HELPFUL HINTS

- Younger players should start closer to the wall.

- As your passing becomes more accurate, start to pass the ball harder.

- Try to spend time passing the ball with your weaker foot.

- When setting yourself targets, only count the passes that hit the wall at the height you aimed for and then returned directly to you. See how many accurate passes you can make from 10 attempts.

P A S S I N G

SHORT PASSES **1**

Stand with the ball 1 metre away from and facing the wall. Pass the ball firmly against the wall, and as it returns, without taking a controlling touch, pass it back against the wall. The practice continues by seeing how many consecutive one-touch passes you can make before you lose control of the ball.

PASS AND TURN **2**

Stand with the ball 1 metre away from and facing the wall. Pass the ball firmly against the wall. When it returns, using only one touch, control the ball so that it stops at your feet. Turn, without the ball, and run quickly to a marker 2 metres behind you. Touch the marker and return to the ball passing it against the wall. The practice continues.

PASS, CONTROL AND PASS **3**

Stand with the ball 2 metres away from and facing the wall. Pass the ball firmly against the wall. When the ball comes back, your controlling touch should set the ball out to your right or left. The second touch, with your other foot, passes the ball back against the wall. The practice continues.

VARIATIONS

- Practise both the passing and control with your weaker foot.
- Try the short passes practice using alternate feet.
- With the short passes practice, try to move parallel with the wall whilst still making pases.
- In the pass and turn practice try controlling the ball, moving backwards to the marker and then forwards to make the next pass.
- In the pass, control and pass practice try using the same foot to control and pass the ball.

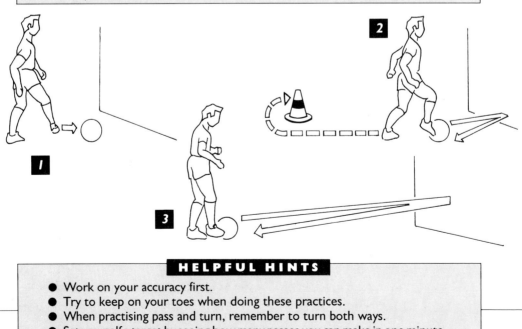

HELPFUL HINTS

- Work on your accuracy first.
- Try to keep on your toes when doing these practices.
- When practising pass and turn, remember to turn both ways.
- Set yourself a target by seeing how many passes you can make in one minute.

P A S S I N G

THE DRIVEN PASS **1**

Stand with the ball at your feet, 10 metres away from and facing the wall. Mark out a target area 1 metre high by 1 metre wide on the wall. Drive the ball firmly at the wall trying to hit the target. Control the ball as it returns and repeat the practice.

THE CHIPPED PASS **2**

Stand with the ball at your feet, 15 metres away from and facing the wall. Chip the ball at the wall trying to hit the 1 metre square target area. Control the ball as it returns and repeat the practice.

THE CURVED PASS **3**

Stand with the ball at your feet, 15 metres away from and facing the wall. Try to make the ball curve as you attempt to hit the target area. Control the ball as it returns and repeat the practice.

VARIATIONS

- Attempt the practices with the ball moving.
- Increase the distance you stand from the wall.
- Mark out the target area on the wall at different heights.
- Place a marker between you and the wall and try to curve the ball around either side of it to hit the target.

HELPFUL HINTS

- Start each practice with the ball completely stationary.

- Select a point on the ball – it may be a panel or part of the brand name. Place the ball so that this point is in the middle of the ball for a driven pass, on one side for a curved pass or between the middle and the bottom half of the ball for a chipped pass.

- At first, concentrate on accuracy not power.

- Set yourself targets – how many times can you hit the target area from 10 attempts?

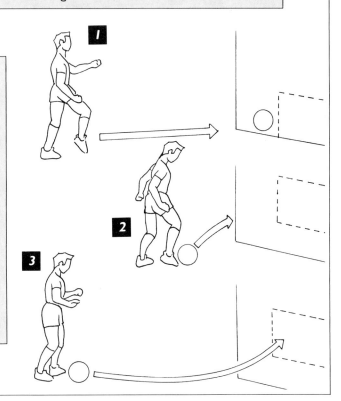

PASSING

BASIC CHIPPING *1*

Mark out an area 10 metres away. Stand with the ball at your feet. The aim is to chip the ball, making it land directly in the target area. Collect the ball and repeat the practice.

CHIPPING OVER SHORT DISTANCES **2**

Mark out an area 3 metres away. Stand with the ball at your feet. Chip the ball as high into the air as possible, making it land and stop directly in the target area. Collect the ball and repeat the practice.

CHIPPING OVER LONG DISTANCES **3**

Mark out an area 15–20 metres away. Stand with the ball at your feet. Chip the ball directly into the target area. Collect the ball and repeat the practice.

VARIATIONS

- Practise with your weaker foot.
- While still trying to land the ball directly into the target areas, try chipping the ball higher into the air.
- Try chipping it lower through the air.
- Try chipping a moving ball.
- Place your foot under the ball and flick it into the target areas.

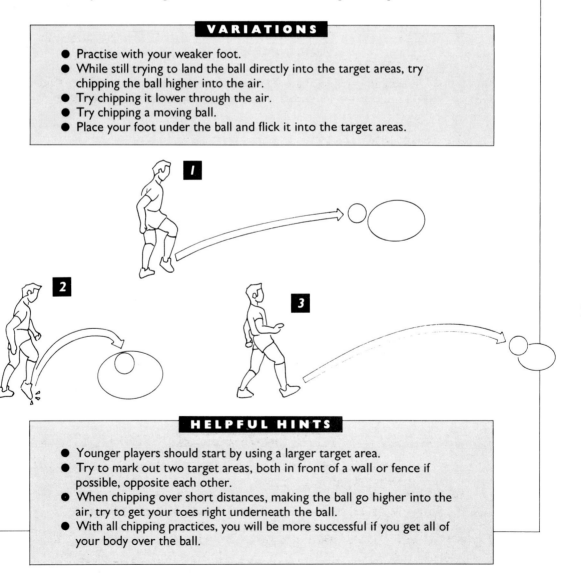

HELPFUL HINTS

- Younger players should start by using a larger target area.
- Try to mark out two target areas, both in front of a wall or fence if possible, opposite each other.
- When chipping over short distances, making the ball go higher into the air, try to get your toes right underneath the ball.
- With all chipping practices, you will be more successful if you get all of your body over the ball.

P A S S I N G

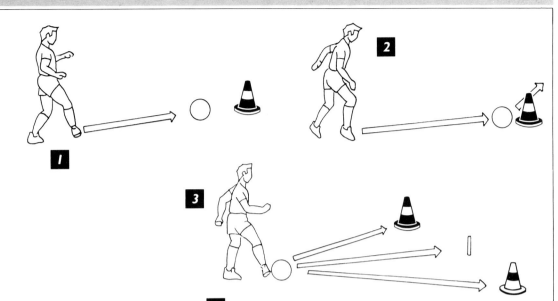

WEIGHTED PASSING **1**

Stand with the ball at your feet. Choose a target more than 10 metres away. Pass the ball so that it stops next to or on the target. Pick out a different target and repeat the practice.

ACCURATE PASSING **2**

Stand with the ball at your feet. Choose a target at least 10 metres away. Pass the ball and try to hit the target. Repeat the practice, trying to hit other targets.

PASSING WITH ACCURACY AND WEIGHT **3**

Choose four or five different targets at various distances away. The object is to hit all of the targets with as few passes as possible. Try again, hitting the targets in the same order, but see if you can reduce the amount of passes it takes.

VARIATIONS

- Practise these passing skills using the inside and outside of the foot.
- Pass the ball firmly. Quickly follow and try to arrive at the target the same time as the ball.
- Select targets where passes have to be played over obstacles.
- Set the ball rolling and whilst it is still moving, attempt these practices.
- Use the weaker foot.

HELPFUL HINTS

- Good passes require accuracy and the right amount of pace. Spend as much time as you can on these practices.
- Try not to select targets that are too far away or too small at first.
- Try to keep the same course and targets so that you can judge your improvement over a period of time.
- Test your best foot against your weakest.

PASSING

WALL PASS **1**

Start 2 metres away from and facing the wall. Keeping the same distance from the wall, play as many one-touch passes as you can against it whilst at the same time walking from one end to the other.

RUNNING WALL PASS **2**

Start 2 metres away from and facing the wall. Play lots of one-touch passes against the wall whilst at the same time running from one end to the other.

OBSTACLE WALL PASS **3**

Place five markers, each 2 metres apart, parallel with the wall. Play first time passes against the wall so that the ball returns to you between the markers. Move from one end of the wall to the other, making passes. Keep the markers between you and the wall.

VARIATIONS

- Try all the passes with the outside of the nearest foot to the wall.
- Try all passes with the inside of the foot furthest from the wall.
- Play the pass firmly against the wall, and then take one touch to control and one to pass.
- Play the first pass half-way up the wall and as it returns, play the next along the ground. Keep playing alternate low and high passes.
- Bring the markers closer together.

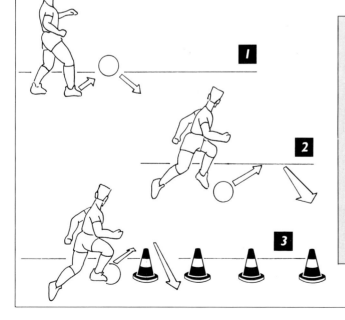

1

2

3

HELPFUL HINTS

- Start the practice further away from the wall.

- Do not introduce the markers until you can move parallel with the wall whilst staying in control of the ball.

- Always try to make these passes so that they return just in front of you.

- Add a competitive edge by seeing how many passes you can make against the wall without losing control.

P A S S I N G

BASIC VOLLEYING **1**

With the ball in your hands, stand 10 metres away from and facing the wall. Drop the ball towards the ground and volley it with the top of your foot at the wall. Control the ball as it returns and repeat the practice.

BASIC HALF-VOLLEYING **2**

With the ball in your hands, stand 10 metres away from and facing the wall. Drop the ball towards the ground. Just as it makes contact with the ground, strike the ball with the top of your foot at the wall. Control the ball as it returns and repeat the practice.

AIRBORNE VOLLEY **3**

With the ball in your hands, stand 10 metres away from and facing the wall. Throw the ball gently up into the air and slightly out in front of you. As it is dropping, jump into the air and volley it with the top of your foot at the wall. Control the ball as it returns and repeat the practice.

V A R I A T I O N S

- As your accuracy improves, increase the distance you stand from the wall.
- Try hitting the ball between the middle and the top to give the volley top spin.
- Throw the ball against the wall and volley or half-volley it back.
- Try flicking the ball up with one foot and volleying it with the other.

H E L P F U L   H I N T S

- Don't try to kick the ball too hard.

- In order to keep the ball low, try and get your body over the ball as you play it.

- With a full volley, allow the ball to nearly hit the ground before playing it.

- Set yourself targets – can you do five consecutive volleys that return directly back to you? Can you do five consecutive half-volleys?

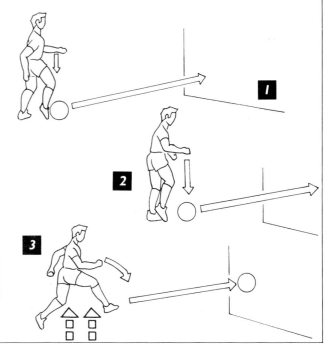

P A S S I N G

GROUND PASSING FOR ACCURACY **1**

Place a marker against the wall. Stand 10 metres away from and in line with the marker, with the ball at your feet. Try to hit the marker with a firm pass.

HALF-VOLLEYING FOR ACCURACY **2**

Place a marker against the wall. Stand 10 metres away from and in line with the marker, holding the ball in your hands. Drop the ball to the ground and strike a half-volley at the marker. Control the ball as it returns and repeat the practice.

VOLLEYING FOR ACCURACY **3**

Place a marker against the wall. Stand 10 metres away from and in line with the marker, holding the ball in your hands. Drop the ball gently and volley it at the marker. Control the ball as it returns and repeat the practice.

VARIATIONS

- Increase and decrease the distance you stand from the wall.
- Use your weaker foot.
- Use the outside of the foot when passing the ball.
- Using alternate feet, keep playing one-touch ground passes at the marker.
- When volleying, try to hit the marker without the ball first touching the ground.

HELPFUL HINTS

- Younger players should start nearer the wall and stand further away as their accuracy improves.

- Concentrate on hitting the markers – increase the power you put into your passes as your accuracy improves.

- Try to spend as much time as possible with this practice. It may seem straightforward but your aim is to hit the marker with every pass.

- Set yourself targets by seeing how many times you can hit the marker from 10 attempts.

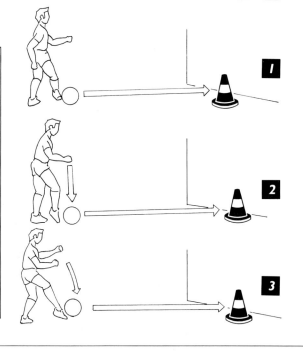

P A S S I N G

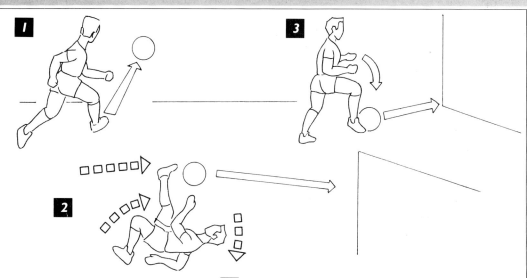

SIDEWAYS-ON VOLLEYING **1**

With the ball in your hands, stand 10 metres away from and sideways-on to the wall. Drop the ball towards the ground and volley it with the top of your foot whilst sideways-on to the wall. Control the ball as it returns and repeat the practice.

SIDE-FOOT VOLLEYING **2**

With the ball in your hands, stand 5 metres away from and facing the wall. Drop the ball towards the ground and volley it with the side of your foot at the wall. Control the ball as it returns and repeat the practice.

BICYCLE KICK **3**

On soft ground, stand 5 metres away from and with your back to the wall holding the ball. Throw the ball gently up into the air. As it drops fall backwards and volley the ball over your head at the wall. Collect the ball and repeat the practice.

VARIATIONS

- Try these practices with your weaker foot.
- Stand 1 metre from the wall and try to make consecutive side-foot volleys without the ball touching the ground.
- Allow the ball to bounce before attempting a volley.
- Try the sideways-on and side-foot practices with a half-volley.
- Place a marker against the wall and try to hit it.

HELPFUL HINTS

- Be patient, these skills are difficult.
- Try to stay on your toes when you do the side-ways on and side-foot practices.
- Start practising the bicycle kick by attempting the volley whilst sitting on the ground.
- Set yourself a target – can you do 10 consecutive side-foot volleys?

Pair
Practices

RUNNING PASSES **1**

The two players move around an area, passing the ball to each other, maintaining a 5-metre distance between them. Each player takes no more than three touches before passing back to their partner. The practice continues using the variations listed below.

HIGH CROSS-FIELD PASSES **2**

The two players, keeping a 20-metre distance between them, move around an area. Whilst on the move, they make high cross-field passes to each other. The receiving player controls the ball and dribbles forward before attempting a return pass which must be played side-ways on to their partner.

VARIATIONS

RUNNING PASSES
- Move more quickly around the area.
- Try this practice using two touches – one to control, the next to pass.
- Practise these passes using the outside of your foot.
- Allow one player only one touch, and the other to play freely.

HIGH CROSS-FIELD PASSES
- Try to curve the high passes.
- Vary the speed and height of the cross-field passes.

P A S S I N G

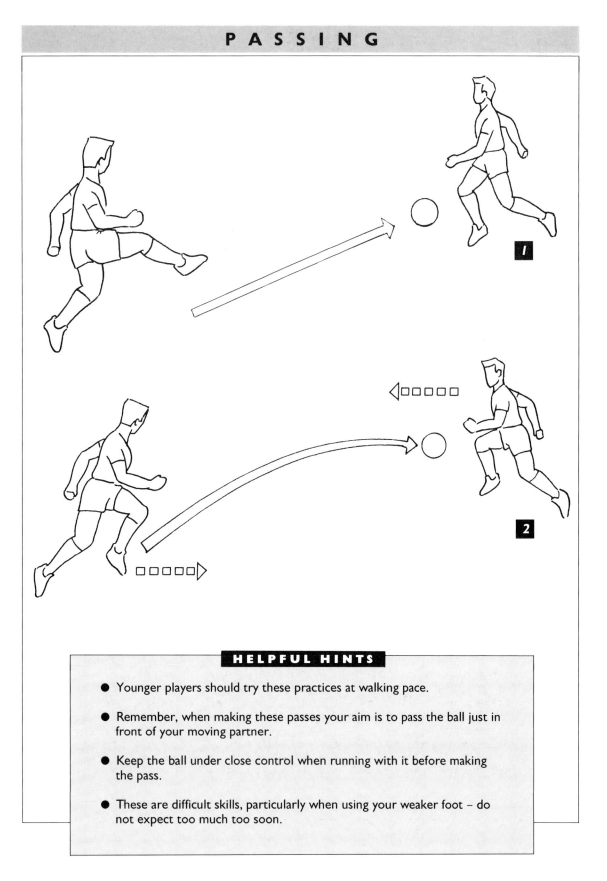

HELPFUL HINTS

● Younger players should try these practices at walking pace.

● Remember, when making these passes your aim is to pass the ball just in front of your moving partner.

● Keep the ball under close control when running with it before making the pass.

● These are difficult skills, particularly when using your weaker foot – do not expect too much too soon.

PASSING

THREE-METRE PASSING █ 1

The player and server stand facing each other 3 metres apart. The server quickly under-arms the ball along the ground to the player, who with only one touch passes the ball back. The practice continues for a minute and the players change roles.

TURN, CONTROL AND PASS █ 2

The player and the server stand facing each other 3 metres apart. The server under-arms the ball over the player's head so that it drops 2 or 3 metres behind the player, who then turns, controls the ball and passes it firmly back. The practice continues with the players changing roles after a period of time.

VARIATIONS

THREE-METRE PASSING
- Serve the ball quicker and allow the player one controlling touch before the return pass.
- Serve the ball towards the player's weaker foot.
- Keeping the ball below waist height, vary the height of the service.

TURN, CONTROL AND PASS
- Serve the ball a few metres further behind the working player for them to control the ball, turn and dribble half-way back before making their pass.
- The working player stands with their back to the server.
- Ask the working player to control the ball and, without turning, back-heel it to the server.

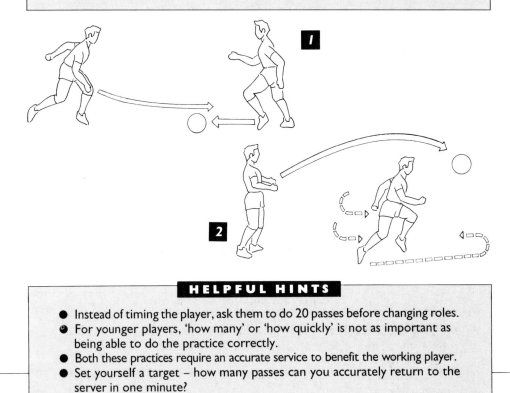

HELPFUL HINTS

- Instead of timing the player, ask them to do 20 passes before changing roles.
- For younger players, 'how many' or 'how quickly' is not as important as being able to do the practice correctly.
- Both these practices require an accurate service to benefit the working player.
- Set yourself a target – how many passes can you accurately return to the server in one minute?

P A S S I N G

PASS AND MOVE BACK **1**

The two players stand 5 metres apart. One player acts as a server and moves forwards dribbling the ball. The working player moves backwards, keeping the 5 metres distance between them. The server passes the ball to the working player who, with only one touch, passes the ball half-way back to the server. The server reaches the ball and passes it first time to the working player who has continued to move backwards. The practice continues with the players changing roles after a set period of time.

PASS AND MOVE **2**

One player, who acts as a server, has the ball and the other player stands 15 metres away. The object of the practice is for the player with the ball to play passes anywhere, within a 15-metre radius, making the receiving player sprint to the ball, have one touch to control it and one to pass back. The players change roles after a set period of time or after a certain amount of passes.

VARIATIONS

PASS AND MOVE BACK
- Ask the player who is moving backwards to pass the ball all the way back to the server.
- The passes must be made with alternate feet.
- Try the practice with both players moving more quickly.

PASS AND MOVE
- Ask the receiving player to pass the ball back without a controlling touch.
- Ask the player receiving to return the ball into the server's hands.
- Ask the player receiving to have three quick touches of the ball before returning it to the server.

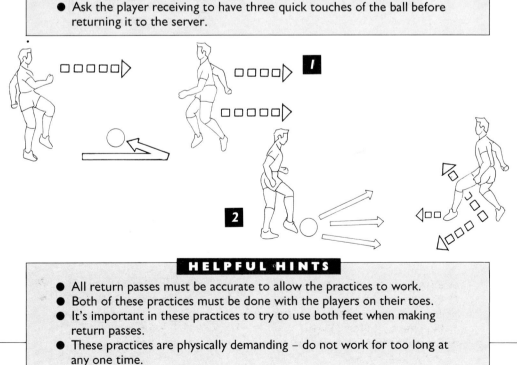

HELPFUL HINTS

- All return passes must be accurate to allow the practices to work.
- Both of these practices must be done with the players on their toes.
- It's important in these practices to try to use both feet when making return passes.
- These practices are physically demanding – do not work for too long at any one time.

P A S S I N G

PASS, TURN AND SPRINT　**1**

The players stand 5 metres apart facing each other. One player acts as a server. Place a marker 5 metres behind the working player. The server passes the ball to the working player, who with only one touch passes it back to the server. The working player then turns, sprints to the marker, touches it, turns again and returns to receive the next pass. The practice continues for a set period of time.

PASS AND REACT　**2**

The two players stand 10 metres apart facing each other. The players make one-touch passes, along the ground, backwards and forwards. After every pass, each player calls out an action that the other player must perform immediately after they have returned the ball. For example, 'JUMP' or 'SIT DOWN'. The practice continues for a set period of time.

◆ VARIATIONS

PASS, TURN AND SPRINT
● Serve the ball under-arm at varying heights.
● Instead of turning, make the player run backwards to the marker.
● Decrease the distance the player has to turn and run to.

PASS AND REACT
● Make the passing distance 15 metres and ask each player to do two different actions each time.
● The players agree on one particular action, e.g. a sit-up. Decreasing the distance between them, they perform it after every pass. Make 10 passes and change the action.

HELPFUL HINTS

● Younger players should be encouraged to have two touches, one to control and the next to pass.
● The service and the return passes must be accurate to make these practices work.
● When trying the Pass, Turn and Sprint practice, players should turn both to the right and to the left.
● To add a competitive element, see how many consecutive, accurate, return passes you can make.

P A S S I N G

ONE-TOUCH PASSING 1

Stand 1 metre away from and facing your partner. Pass the ball to your partner and with only one touch they must pass the ball back. The practice continues with the ball going backwards and forwards until a pass is misplaced.

TWO-TOUCH PASSING 2

Stand with a ball at your feet 10 metres away from and facing your partner. Pass the ball firmly along the ground to your partner. With only one controlling touch, the receiving player sets the ball slightly out in front of them and with the second touch passes the ball firmly back. The practice continues.

VARIATIONS

ONE-TOUCH PASSING
- Use alternate feet when passing the ball.
- Keeping I metre apart, one player moves forward, while the other moves backwards.

TWO-TOUCH PASSING
- Try to make your controlling touch set the ball out I metre either side of you before passing the ball back.
- Use the outside of the foot to control the ball before passing it back.
- Receive the pass with one foot, moving it across for the other foot to make the pass back.

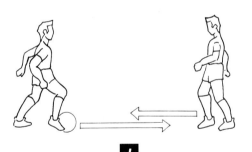

1

HELPFUL HINTS

- When doing these practices, the players should be alert and on their toes.

- When starting, younger players should concentrate on passing accurately along the ground.

- It's important in the one-touch practice to maintain the I metre distance between the two players.

- With the one-touch practice, see how many passes you can make in one minute.

- With the two-touch practice, see how many consecutive passes you can make between you.

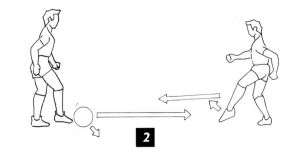

2

PASSING

LONG PASSING GAME 1

The two players stand 25 metres apart, each behind their own goal which is 3 metres wide. The player in possession of the ball tries to pass the ball through their opponent's goal. The opposing player controls the ball and then attempts to do the same. Both players must stay behind their own goal. The first player to score 10 goals wins the game.

SHORT PASSING GAME 2

The two players stand 5 metres apart behind their own goal which is 1 metre wide. The player in possession of the ball tries to pass it through their opponent's goal. The opposing player, without taking a controlling touch, tries to do the same. The game continues with each player passing the ball backwards and forwards with one touch. Each player starts with 10 points and every time a player fails to pass the ball through the goal a point is lost. The first player to lose all 10 points loses the game.

VARIATIONS

LONG PASSING GAME
● Try to pass the ball between the goal without it first touching the ground.

● Allow the receiving player only one touch to control and the next to pass.

● Play this game using volleys and half-volleys to try to score. Allow players to pick the ball up.

SHORT PASSING GAME
● Make first time passes with alternate feet.

● Increase the distance between the two goals.

COMBINED
● Try the practices with your weakest foot.

P A S S I N G

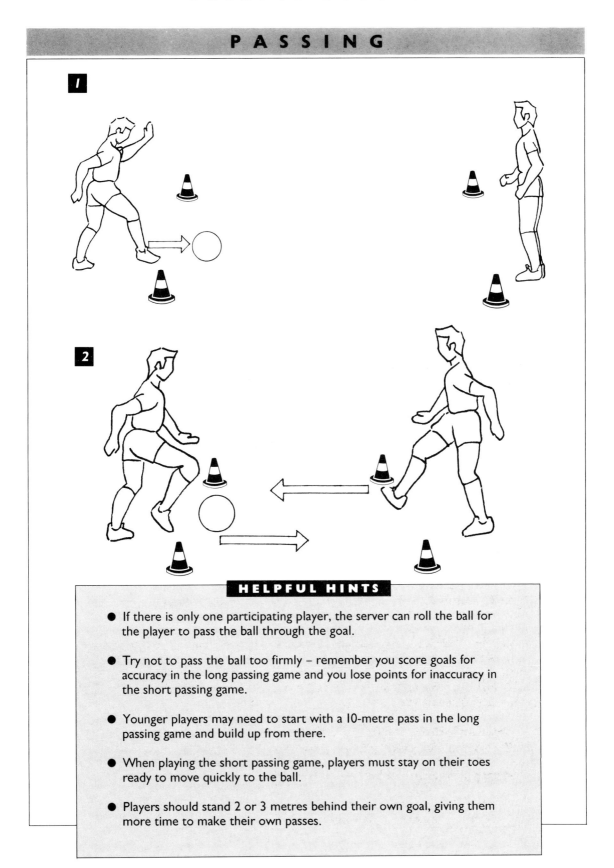

1

2

HELPFUL HINTS

● If there is only one participating player, the server can roll the ball for the player to pass the ball through the goal.

● Try not to pass the ball too firmly – remember you score goals for accuracy in the long passing game and you lose points for inaccuracy in the short passing game.

● Younger players may need to start with a 10-metre pass in the long passing game and build up from there.

● When playing the short passing game, players must stay on their toes ready to move quickly to the ball.

● Players should stand 2 or 3 metres behind their own goal, giving them more time to make their own passes.

P A S S I N G

PASS TO SCORE   **1**

The two players stand facing each other 20 metres apart with a goal 3 metres wide between them. The players take turns to try to pass the ball through the goal. They must not come within 10 metres of the goal and the pass must reach their partner. The practice continues with each player trying to pass the ball through the goal.

PASS AND HIT   **2**

The two players stand 15 metres apart behind a marker. The object of the practice is for each player to pass the ball along the ground to try to hit their partner's marker. The players must allow the ball to travel past the marker before controlling it and continuing with the practice.

VARIATIONS

PASS TO SCORE
- Increase and decrease the distance to the goal.
- Try passing the ball through the markers without it touching the ground.
- Make the goal smaller.

PASS AND HIT
- Increase the distance between the markers.
- Try to hit the marker without the ball first touching the ground.

COMBINED
- Try taking just two touches – one to control, the next to pass.
- Try using your weaker foot.

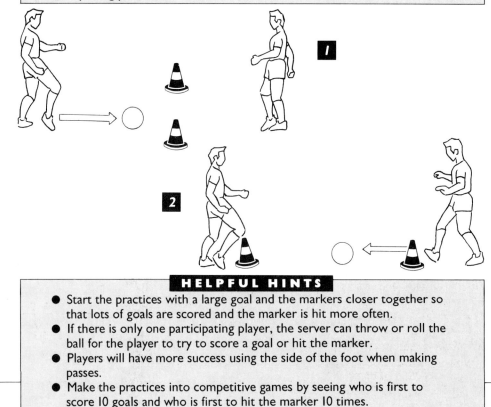

HELPFUL HINTS

- Start the practices with a large goal and the markers closer together so that lots of goals are scored and the marker is hit more often.
- If there is only one participating player, the server can throw or roll the ball for the player to try to score a goal or hit the marker.
- Players will have more success using the side of the foot when making passes.
- Make the practices into competitive games by seeing who is first to score 10 goals and who is first to hit the marker 10 times.

P A S S I N G

WALL BALL **1**

Mark out a goal 3 metres wide on the wall. The two players stand 10 metres away from and facing the wall. The object of the game is for the two players, in turn, to pass the ball first time into the goal. The game continues until one player misses the goal and loses the game. The losing player starts the next game.

TARGET BALL **2**

Mark out a circle, 1 metre off the ground on the wall, as a target. The two players stand 10 metres away from and facing the wall. The player in possession tries to pass the ball to hit the target. If the pass misses, the other player, without first taking a controlling touch, attempts to hit the target. The game continues until the target is hit, with the losing player starting the next game.

VARIATIONS

WALL BALL
● Increase and decrease the width of the goal.

TARGET BALL
● Mark the target higher up the wall and allow a controlling touch before attempting the pass.

COMBINED
● Try these practices with your weaker foot.
● Try these practices using only side-foot passes.

HELPFUL HINTS

● Younger players can play wall ball by seeing how many consecutive passes they and their partner can play between them against the wall before they lose control of the ball.

● When playing wall ball, try to trick your opponent by pretending to pass it to one side of the goal and then quickly passing it to the other.

● Likewise, when waiting to receive the ball, try to guess where the ball will rebound to when it comes off the wall.

● As soon as you have made your pass, move back away from the wall positioning yourself to receive the next pass.

● When playing target ball, the pace of the pass is important – not too quickly to miss the target but not too slowly to give your opponent a chance to score.

● To make these games more competitive, see which player is first to win 10 games – five wall ball followed by five target ball.

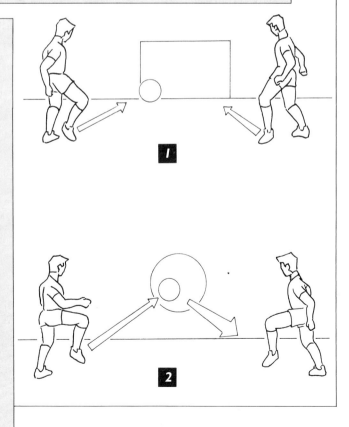

PASSING

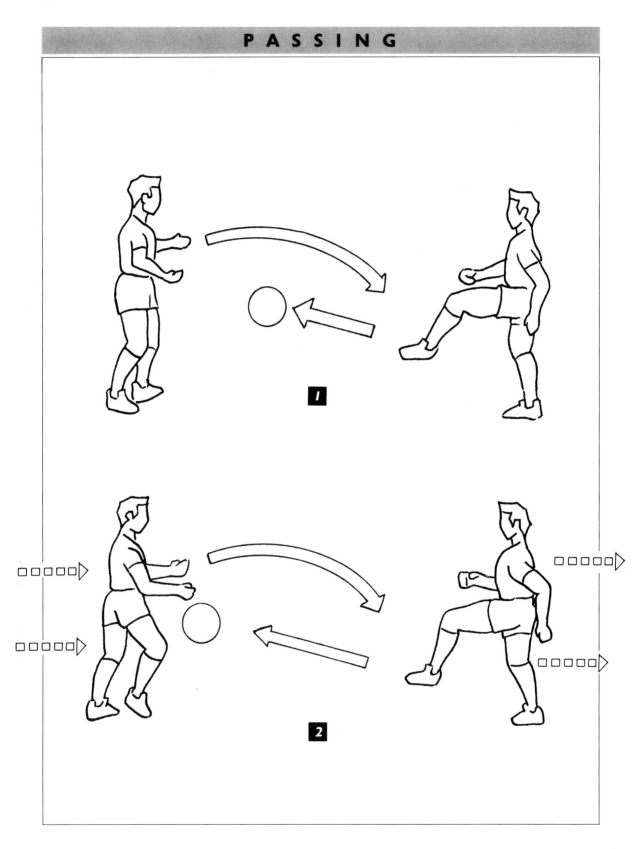

P A S S I N G

STATIONARY VOLLEYS AND HALF-VOLLEYS **1**

The two players stand facing each other 2 metres apart. The server throws the ball for the working player to volley or half-volley back. The practice continues with the players changing roles after a period of time.

MOVING VOLLEYS OR HALF-VOLLEYS **2**

The two players stand facing each other 2 metres apart, with the server holding the ball. Simultaneously the server moves forwards and the working player moves backwards. Whilst on the move the server throws the ball to the working player who volleys or half-volleys it back. The practice continues with the players changing roles after a set distance or period of time.

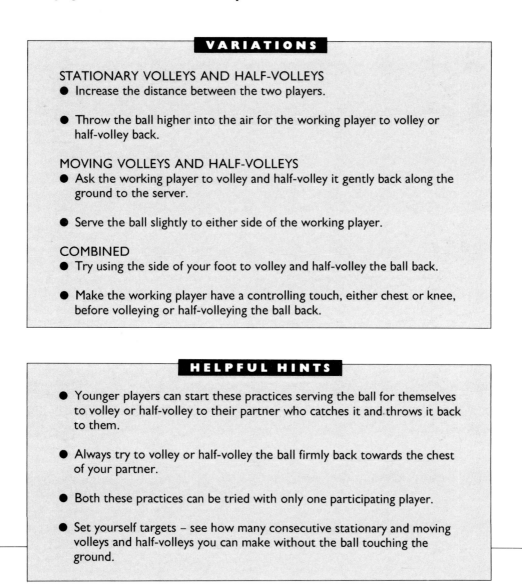

VARIATIONS

STATIONARY VOLLEYS AND HALF-VOLLEYS
- Increase the distance between the two players.

- Throw the ball higher into the air for the working player to volley or half-volley back.

MOVING VOLLEYS AND HALF-VOLLEYS
- Ask the working player to volley and half-volley it gently back along the ground to the server.

- Serve the ball slightly to either side of the working player.

COMBINED
- Try using the side of your foot to volley and half-volley the ball back.

- Make the working player have a controlling touch, either chest or knee, before volleying or half-volleying the ball back.

HELPFUL HINTS

- Younger players can start these practices serving the ball for themselves to volley or half-volley to their partner who catches it and throws it back to them.

- Always try to volley or half-volley the ball firmly back towards the chest of your partner.

- Both these practices can be tried with only one participating player.

- Set yourself targets – see how many consecutive stationary and moving volleys and half-volleys you can make without the ball touching the ground.

Group Practices

PASSING

NUMBER OF PLAYERS

4 or more.

EQUIPMENT

One ball between four players.

PLAYING AREA

50 metres by 20 metres.

THE PRACTICE

Divide the players into fours with one ball between them. Mark out a 20 metres by 10 metres area, and 15 metres away on either side place two markers 20 metres apart. One player stands between the markers at either end, and the other two are positioned in the 20 by 10 area. One of the two players in this area acts as a defender.

The object of the practice is for the players at either end to try to pass the ball along the ground to each other through the middle area, directly or with the help of the middle player. The middle defender tries to stop the passes, by intercepting the ball or tackling the middle player. The middle players must stay inside their area, and the end players can only move across the imaginary line between their two markers. After a set period of time the players change roles.

VARIATIONS

- Allow the middle player to pass the ball back to the player they have just received a pass from.

- Only allow the middle player two touches, one to control, the other for the pass.

- Decrease the passing distance for the two outside players and ask both the middle players to try and intercept their passes.

- Allow passes to be made above head height, and let the defenders use their hands. The players receiving passes must control the ball by using their feet, thighs and chest.

P A S S I N G

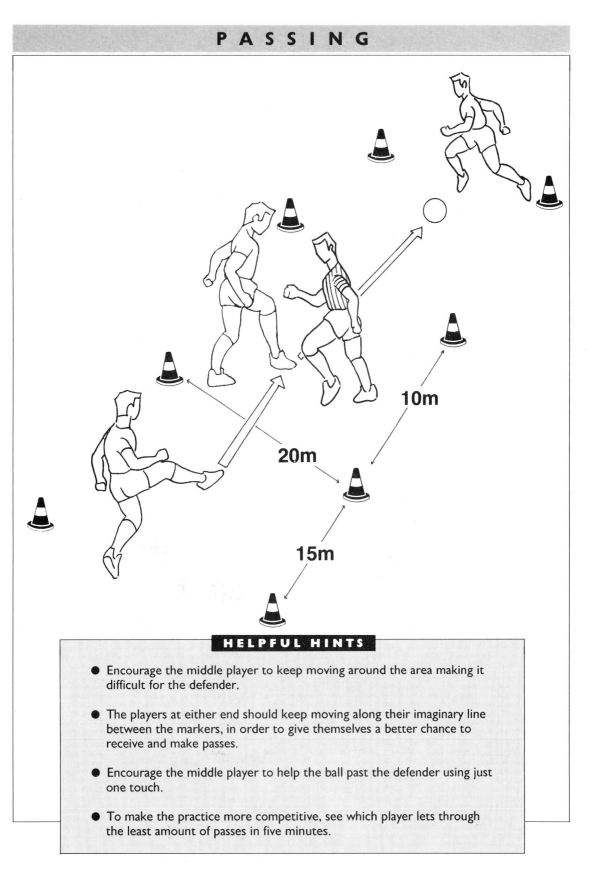

10m

20m

15m

HELPFUL HINTS

● Encourage the middle player to keep moving around the area making it difficult for the defender.

● The players at either end should keep moving along their imaginary line between the markers, in order to give themselves a better chance to receive and make passes.

● Encourage the middle player to help the ball past the defender using just one touch.

● To make the practice more competitive, see which player lets through the least amount of passes in five minutes.

PASSING

NUMBER OF PLAYERS

6 or more.

EQUIPMENT

One ball, bibs and markers.

PLAYING AREA

40 metres by 30 metres.

THE PRACTICE

Divide the players into two equal teams. Mark out two goals 15 metres wide at either end of the playing area. The object of the practice is for each team to try and score by passing the ball along the ground through the goal. When the ball goes out of the playing area, the team who have possession restart the game by passing it back in from the side line, and when it goes out over the goal line, pass it back into the playing area from that point.

VARIATIONS

- Restrict the players to having only two touches.
- Make the players have three touches before they are allowed to make a pass.
- Players are only allowed to score when they are over the half-way line.
- All passes must be made below waist height.
- Goals can only be scored when all of the attacking team are in their opponents' half.

HELPFUL HINTS

- Encourage players to use all of the playing area and to keep on the move.
- Do not have more than six players in each team.
- When scoring becomes too easy, decrease the size of the goal.
- Award an extra goal if a team makes seven consecutive passes.

PASSING

NUMBER OF PLAYERS

5 or more.

EQUIPMENT

One ball and markers.

PLAYING AREA

60 metres by 60 metres.

THE PRACTICE

The players are divided into groups of five. Mark out a square 3 metres by 3 metres, with one player positioned inside. The other four players are positioned 30 metres away around the outside of the square. The object of the practice is for the players around the outside to pass the ball firmly into the square to the middle player, who must control it inside that area. The middle player passes the ball back to any of the outside players and the practice continues.

VARIATIONS

- Give each of the four outside players a ball.

- Ask the players to firmly pass the ball through the air to the middle player.

- Allow players to vary the distance they stand from the square.

- Encourage players to make curved and chipped passes or pick the ball up to play volleys and half-volleys to the middle player.

- Ask the outside players to roll the ball forward and make their pass with a moving ball.

HELPFUL HINTS

- Younger players should start closer to the square.

- Concentrate on accuracy before any of the passing variations are tried.

- See which of the four outside players makes 10 consecutive accurate passes first.

- Only count a pass as successful when the player in the middle controls the ball inside the square.

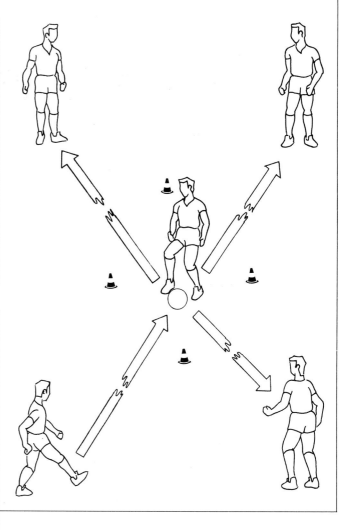

P A S S I N G

NUMBER OF PLAYERS
8 or more.

EQUIPMENT
One ball and bibs, and markers.

PLAYING AREA
40 metres by 40 metres.

THE PRACTICE
Divide the players into two equal teams. Position the markers anywhere around the playing area. The markers must be two different colours (a coloured bib could be placed over half the markers). The object of this practice is for the team in possession to try to pass the ball to hit their designated coloured markers. When possession is lost, by either an intercepted pass or tackle, the other team then tries to hit their coloured markers. Each team has the same amount of markers to hit.

VARIATIONS

- Ask players to play a long pass after every two or three short passes.

- Make each team pass at the other set of coloured markers.

- See which team is the first to hit five markers, regardless of the colour.

- Allow each team to hit their own markers, thereby taking one 'goal' off their opponents' score.

- Ask one team to defend all of the markers, while the other tries to hit them.

- Only allow a score to count if the pass that hits the marker was made from more than 5 metres away.

P A S S I N G

HELPFUL HINTS

● Always have more markers than players.

● Never have more than eight players in each team.

● If you have 20 players, either play two separate games or divide the players into three teams with one team resting whilst the other two play against each other.

● Encourage the players to use all of the playing area, by playing long and short passes.

● Set a time limit and see which team hits the markers the most.

P A S S I N G

NUMBER OF PLAYERS

5 or more.

EQUIPMENT

One ball per group and markers.

PLAYING AREA

10 metres by 10 metres.

THE PRACTICE

Divide the players into groups of five. Mark out an area 10 metres square and position four players, one on each side of the square. The fifth player stands inside the square. The object of the practice is for the four outside players to pass the ball along the ground to each other without the player in the middle intercepting it. The players on the outside can move both ways along their own imaginary line but must not come into the square. The practice continues for a set period of time with each player taking turns to be the middle player.

VARIATIONS

- Allow the players two touches, one to control and the next to pass.
- Use only three players on three lines of the square.
- Allow players to move anywhere around the square, whilst keeping on the lines.
- Do not allow the players around the outside of the square to stop the ball.
- Do not allow the player in possession to pass it to a player directly opposite.
- Make the playing area larger and introduce another player in the middle.

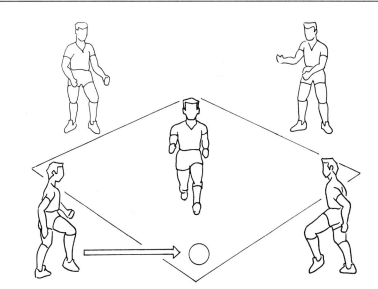

HELPFUL HINTS

- Younger players should start with a larger area.
- Encourage players to move along their lines, to make it easier for the player with the ball to pass to them.
- All of the passes in this practice should be made with the inside of the foot.
- To make the practice more competitive, see which group of players around the square make the most consecutive passes.

P A S S I N G

NUMBER OF PLAYERS

6 or more.

EQUIPMENT

One ball between two players.

PLAYING AREA

20 metres by 20 metres.

THE PRACTICE

Divide the players into pairs with a ball between them. The object of the practice is for the players to pass the ball to each other whilst moving around the playing area. The passes should be played along the ground and reach their partner without touching another player or ball. The players must keep on the move and always be at least 5 metres apart.

VARIATIONS

- Encourage the players to dribble past or around any player from another pair when in possession of the ball and before making a pass.
- Ask the players to pass the ball into a space to allow their partner to run onto it.
- Ask the players to turn sharply when receiving a pass, and to dribble off in a new direction before making their own pass.
- Ask the players to dribble towards their partner instead of passing, allowing them to take possession.

HELPFUL HINTS

- Passes should be made firmly with the side of the foot.

- Make the practice more demanding by decreasing the size of the playing area.

- With younger players make the area larger to avoid the players getting in each other's way.

- Encourage players to call for the ball when they wish their partner to pass to them.

- Encourage players only to pass when they can clearly see their partner.

PASSING

NUMBER OF PLAYERS
6 or more.

EQUIPMENT
3 balls between six players.

PLAYING AREA
30 metres by 30 metres.

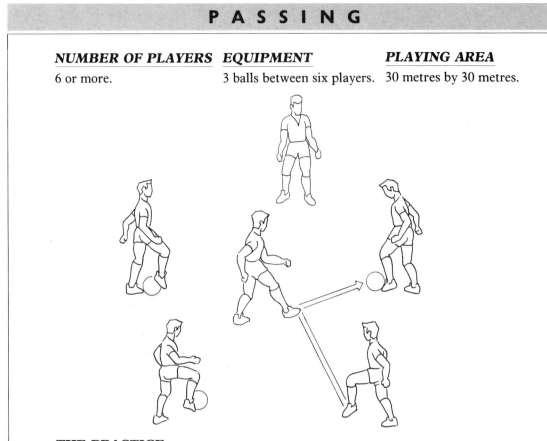

THE PRACTICE

The players are divided into groups of six, and form a circle 15 metres across with one player standing in the middle. One of the players with a ball passes it in to the middle player who, with only one touch, passes it to any other player not in possession of a ball. The practice continues with any one of the players in possession of a ball passing it into the middle player.

VARIATIONS

- Give all but one of the outside players a ball.
- Vary the height and pace of the service.
- Allow the player in the middle to have two touches – one to control and the other to pass.
- Increase and decrease the size of the circle.
- Add more players to the circle and have two players in the middle.

HELPFUL HINTS

- With younger players start the practice with just one ball.
- To ensure the middle player knows where the next pass is coming from, encourage the outside players to call when they make their pass.
- In order to make this practice more competitive, ask the player in the middle to count how many passes they can make in one minute.
- If the middle player passes the ball to an outside player already in possession, give them a fun punishment at the end of the minute.

P A S S I N G

NUMBER OF PLAYERS

8 or more.

EQUIPMENT

One ball, markers and bibs.

PLAYING AREA

40 metres by 40 metres.

THE PRACTICE

Divide the players into two equal teams. Place four or five goals, 2 metres wide, around the playing area. The object of the practice is for a player to pass the ball along the ground and through any of the goals to another member of their team. If the ball touches an opposing player the 'goal' is disallowed. When the opposing team gain possession they also try to score by passing through the goals. The team in possession are allowed to retain the ball after scoring a goal and only lose possession if the opposition win the ball or force it out of the playing area.

VARIATIONS

- Only allow a goal to count when the ball has been passed through the goal and returned with one touch back to the passing player.
- Do not allow the players to try and score until they have made five consecutive passes.
- Allow players to score by dribbling the ball through the goals.
- Only allow a 'goal' to count when passes have been made through two different goals.

HELPFUL HINTS

- Do not allow players to act as goalkeepers by standing between the markers on the imaginary goal line.

- Position the goals well apart, and at various angles to each other.

- Only allow a 'goal' to count when the receiving player has the ball under control.

- Make the practice more competitive by seeing which team is the first to score 10 goals.

PASSING

NUMBER OF PLAYERS
4 or more.

EQUIPMENT
One ball between 4.

PLAYING AREA
20 metres by 10 metres.

THE PRACTICE
Divide the players into two sets of pairs and position them 20 metres apart. The first player passes the ball firmly along the ground to either of the players opposite. The receiving player, with only one touch, plays the ball to their partner who again, with only one touch, plays it back to either one of the players opposite. This receiving player plays it to their partner and the practice continues.

VARIATIONS

- Ask the players to pass the ball through the air to the player opposite.
- Allow the player receiving the long pass to have two touches, the first to control and the next to pass.
- Decrease and increase the distance between the pairs.
- Decrease and increase the distance between the two players in the pair.
- Ask the receiving player to play the ball to their partner, get it back, and make the pass to either of the players opposite.

HELPFUL HINTS

- Younger players can have more controlling touches of the ball to ensure their passes are more accurate.
- Start the practice by passing the ball between the pairs at a gentler pace to allow the players to be in control and more accurate with their passing.
- As this is a stationary practice, ensure players are on their toes and concentrating.
- Start the players in the pair further apart and as their control improves bring them closer together.
- Encourage players to use both feet when making their passes.

P A S S I N G

NUMBER OF PLAYERS

6 or more.

EQUIPMENT

One ball and bibs.

PLAYING AREA

30 metres by 30 metres.

THE PRACTICE

Divide the players into two equal teams with one wearing bibs. The object of the practice is for both teams to try and retain possession of the ball. The team not in possession try to win the ball by intercepting a pass, making a tackle or forcing the ball out of the playing area. When the ball goes out of the playing area, the team whose possession it now is restart the practice by rolling it back in.

VARIATIONS

- Restrict the players to no more than two touches, one to control and the next to pass.
- Ask players to touch the ball three times before making their pass.
- Only allow passes to be played below head height.
- Players can only win possession of the ball by intercepting passes or by forcing the ball to be played outside the playing area.
- Ask the players to play at least one long pass to every five short passes.

HELPFUL HINTS

- If the teams are easily retaining possession, make the playing area smaller. Likewise make the area larger allowing them more space to pass the ball, if retaining possession is difficult.
- Do not have more than six players in each team.
- Encourage the players to use all the playing area, making both long and short passes.
- To make the practice more competitive, award a goal for 10 consecutive passes. For younger players, set a lower target.
- See which team makes the most consecutive passes by the end of the practice.

P A S S I N G

NUMBER OF PLAYERS
3 or more.

EQUIPMENT
One ball between 3 players, and markers.

PLAYING AREA
40 metres by 15 metres.

THE PRACTICE
The players are divided into groups of three with a ball between them. One player stands in the middle between two markers positioned 15 metres apart. On either side, 20 metres away from the middle player and also standing between markers 15 metres apart, are the two other players. All three players must stay on an imaginary line between their markers. The object of the practice is for the two outside players to try and pass the ball along the ground and between the middle markers to each other. The player in the middle can intercept the pass but cannot handle the ball. The practice continues with players changing roles after a set period of time.

VARIATIONS

- Increase and decrease the width between the markers in the middle.
- Allow the middle player to handle the ball.
- Only allow the players at either end to have one controlling touch and the next to make their pass.
- Allow the middle player to change places with the player whose pass they have intercepted.
- Allow passes to go above head height and let the middle player use hands to try and intercept. Do not allow the outside players to use their hands when controlling these passes.

HELPFUL HINTS

- With younger players, shorten the passing distance.

- Passes should be played firmly, but the player at the other end of the playing area must be able to control it without using their hands.

- Try to trick the player in the middle by looking to pass the ball to one side of this player, but playing it to the other.

- Add a competitive element by seeing which player achieves the most successful number of passes from 10 attempts.

P A S S I N G

NUMBER OF PLAYERS
6 or more.

EQUIPMENT
A ball.

PLAYING AREA
20 metres by 20 metres.

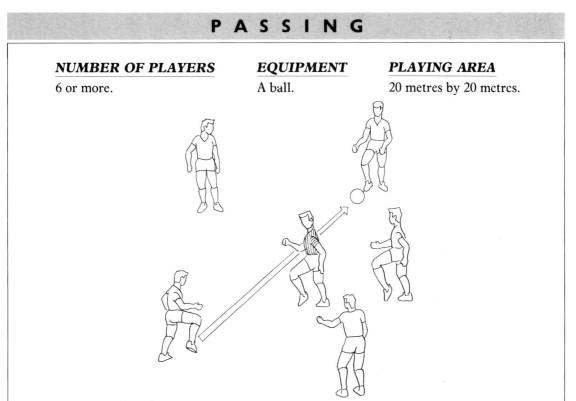

THE PRACTICE

The players form a circle with one player standing in the middle. The object of the practice is for the players to pass the ball around and across the circle, whilst the player in the middle tries to intercept. If there is an interception, or the ball goes outside the circle, the player who last made contact with the ball changes places with the player in the middle.

VARIATIONS

- Try the practice with two players in the middle.
- Ask the players forming the circle to only have one touch.
- Add another ball.
- Restrict the players from passing to the players directly on either side of them.
- Ask the players forming the circle to take two touches, using one foot to control the ball and the other to pass.

HELPFUL HINTS

- Start the practice with a big circle.
- Decrease the size of the circle as the players' passing improves.
- Do not allow the same player to stay in the middle for too long.
- Encourage players to move sideways, but do not allow them to come into the circle to control or make a pass.
- To add a competitive element, see if the players forming the circle can make 10 passes.
- If you have two players in the middle, and a pass goes between them, make the middle two players intercept the ball twice before they can leave the middle.

PASSING

NUMBER OF PLAYERS

3 or more.

EQUIPMENT

One ball between 3 players and markers.

PLAYING AREA

20 metres by 20 metres.

THE PRACTICE

The players are divided into threes. One of the three players acts as the defender of an imaginary goal-line between two markers 10 metres apart. The other two are attacking players. One of these attacking players stands immediately in front of the defender on their goal line. The other attacking player, in possession of the ball, starts 20 metres away from the goal line opposite. This player starts the practice by passing the ball to the other attacker. The object of the practice is for the two attackers, by passing the ball between them, to score a goal by stopping the ball on the defender's goal line. If the ball is won by the defender or goes out of the playing area, the practice is restarted. Each of the players takes a turn at being the defender and the practice continues.

VARIATIONS

- Ask the serving player to vary the height and pace of the first pass.

- Place two markers 5 metres apart on the goal line and ask the two attackers to try to pass the ball through them to score.

- Ask the attacking player receiving the starting pass to touch the ball five times before either scoring or passing.

- Incorporate the offside rule into the practice. If either of the attacking players receive a pass in an offside position, the 'goal' does not count.

P A S S I N G

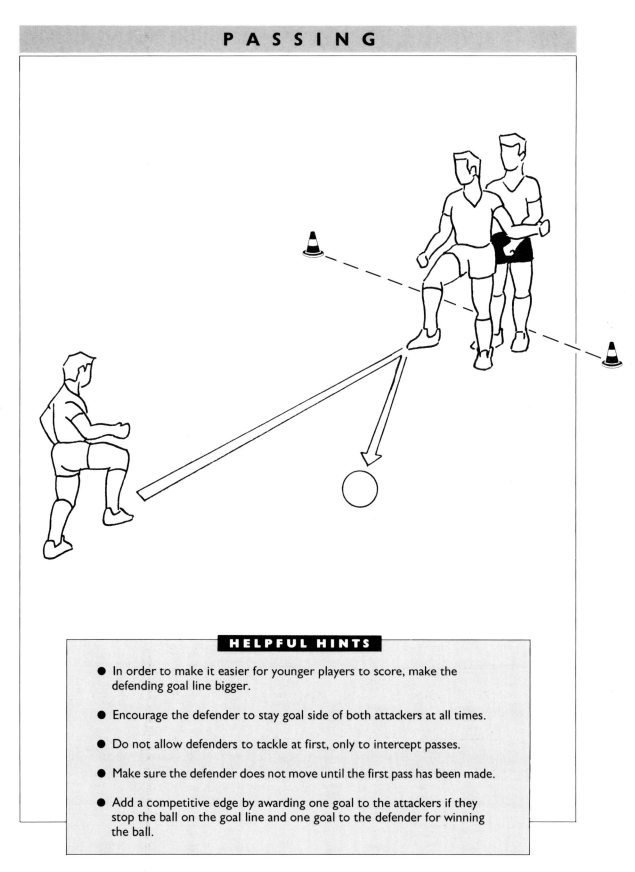

HELPFUL HINTS

● In order to make it easier for younger players to score, make the defending goal line bigger.

● Encourage the defender to stay goal side of both attackers at all times.

● Do not allow defenders to tackle at first, only to intercept passes.

● Make sure the defender does not move until the first pass has been made.

● Add a competitive edge by awarding one goal to the attackers if they stop the ball on the goal line and one goal to the defender for winning the ball.

P A S S I N G

NUMBER OF PLAYERS
7 or more.

EQUIPMENT
One ball and markers.

PLAYING AREA
20 metres by 40 metres.

THE PRACTICE
Divide the players into teams of three. The players in each team stand behind each other in a line so that two lines of players face each other 40 metres apart. A receiving player is positioned at the mid-point between the two lines and on either side of this player, 20 metres away, there are two markers. The first player in the line passes the ball along the ground to the player in the middle and runs to the marker on the right. The ball is returned to the passing player who then plays it to the first player in the line opposite. The player who started the practice joins the back of the other team and the practice continues.

VARIATIONS

- Ask the players to pass the ball to the middle player and then run to the marker on the left.
- Make all the passes one touch.
- Bring the markers closer to the middle player.
- Ask the players in the lines to make their passes through the air.

HELPFUL HINTS

- After the players have received the ball back from the middle player, encourage them to take a controlling touch before making their next pass.
- Keep changing the player in the middle.
- Encourage the players to make firm, accurate passes with the side of their foot as quickly as they can.
- If you have a large number of players, add another player in the middle and another ball.

P A S S I N G

NUMBER OF PLAYERS
6 or more.

EQUIPMENT
One ball between 4.

PLAYING AREA
10 metres by 10 metres.

THE PRACTICE
Divide the players into groups of six with one ball between them. The players form a circle. The object of the practice is for the players to pass the ball across the circle and immediately follow their pass. The receiving player controls the ball and passes to another player in the circle, again following the pass. The practice continues with each player in turn passing the ball and taking the place of the receiving player.

VARIATIONS

- Ask the players to pass the ball through the air across the circle.
- Ask the players to pass the ball across the circle, receive a return pass and then pass it back to the receiving player.
- Ask the players to pass the ball across the circle, receive a return pass and then pass it to a different player.
- Ask the players to pass across the circle then run around the outside of the circle to take the place of the receiving player.

HELPFUL HINTS

- If you have a large number of players, form more than one circle.
- Make the practice more demanding by decreasing the size of the circle.
- Do not allow the players to pass the ball to the players either side of them.
- All the players should be alert and on their toes ready to receive a pass.

PASSING

NUMBER OF PLAYERS

12 or more.

EQUIPMENT

One ball per team.

PLAYING AREA

20 metres by 20 metres.

THE PRACTICE

The players are divided into four teams. The players in each team stand behind each other in a line. The four teams form a square. The player in possession of the ball passes it along the ground to the first player in any of the other three teams. Immediately after passing the ball this player follows the pass and joins the back of that line. The receiving player controls the ball and passes it to the first player in any of the other three lines and the practice continues.

VARIATIONS

- Ask the teams to form a rectangle – the players will then have the option of short square passes or long, straight and diagonal passes.

- Number the teams 1–4. The player who passes the ball calls out a number. The receiving player must then play the ball to that team and call out another number.

- Ask the players to pass the ball and quickly join the back of their own team.

- Ask the players to make all their passes with their weakest foot.

- Ask the players to pass the ball first time.

P A S S I N G

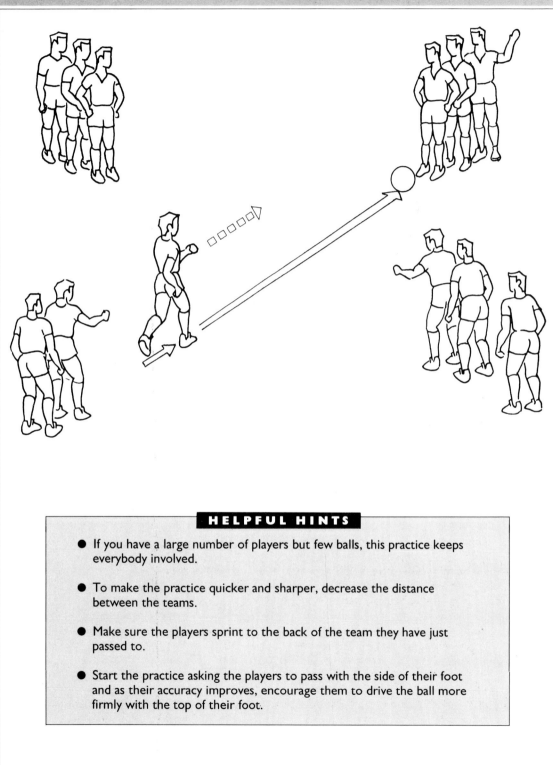

HELPFUL HINTS

● If you have a large number of players but few balls, this practice keeps everybody involved.

● To make the practice quicker and sharper, decrease the distance between the teams.

● Make sure the players sprint to the back of the team they have just passed to.

● Start the practice asking the players to pass with the side of their foot and as their accuracy improves, encourage them to drive the ball more firmly with the top of their foot.

PASSING

NUMBER OF PLAYERS

3 or more.

EQUIPMENT

Two balls between 3 players.

PLAYING AREA

20 metres by 10 metres.

THE PRACTICE

Organise the players into groups of three with one player in the middle and the other two five metres away on either side. The two outside players have a ball each. These players, in turn, pass the ball to the player in the middle who passes it back and turns to receive a pass from the other serving player. After a period of one minute, the players change rôles and the practice continues.

VARIATIONS

- The outside players, using their hands, throw the ball waist high for the middle player to volley back.
- The outside players vary the height and pace of the service, making the middle player control the ball before passing it back.
- The outside players serve the ball into the middle player through the air and ask the middle player to keep the ball off the ground with three touches before returning their pass.
- The middle player passes the ball back to the server and then sprints around the back of this player before receiving the next serve from the other outside player.

HELPFUL HINTS

- The service to the player in the middle must be accurate.
- Encourage the outside players to call the middle player's name when they serve the ball in.
- To keep the middle player working, if one ball is misplaced, keep serving from the same side until the ball is retrieved.
- To add a competitive edge, see how many passes the middle player can make in one minute.

PASSING

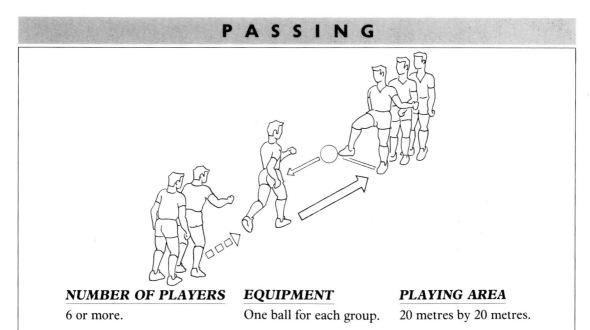

NUMBER OF PLAYERS
6 or more.

EQUIPMENT
One ball for each group.

PLAYING AREA
20 metres by 20 metres.

THE PRACTICE

The players are divided into two teams. The players in each team stand behind each other in a line. The two lines of players face each other at least 10 metres apart. The first player in the line has the ball and passes it along the ground to the player opposite. The passing player immediately follows the pass, running straight towards the receiving player. This will force the receiving player, when controlling the ball, to take it either to the left or the right of the oncoming player before returning the pass and immediately following it. The player who made the first pass joins the end of the line opposite. The practice continues.

VARIATIONS

- Ask the players to chip or drive the passes to the player opposite.
- Ask the receiving player to control the pass with the first touch and return the pass with the next.
- Ask the player who has passed the ball and followed it to become a defender who is not allowed to tackle but can try to intercept the return pass.
- Ask the players to pass the ball with their weaker foot.
- Ask the players to use the outside of the foot to control the ball before making their return pass.

HELPFUL HINTS

- For younger players, increase the distance between the two lines of players, giving the receiving player more time.
- Make sure the receiving players do not take the ball too wide before making their return pass.
- All passes should be made with the side of the foot to ensure accuracy.
- Remember this is a passing practice – the aim is to return the ball quickly and accurately to the player opposite. Do not encourage players to dribble past the defender, but to pass around them.

PASSING

NUMBER OF PLAYERS

6 or more.

EQUIPMENT

One ball between 6 players, and markers.

PLAYING AREA

20 metres by 20 metres.

THE PRACTICE

Divide the players into groups of six with one ball between them. Position a player on each of the four corners of the 20 metre by 20 metre area. The two remaining players – one acting as an attacker, the other as a defender – are positioned in the middle. The object of this practice is for the attacking player to receive and return passes with any of the four players on the corners, while the defender tries to intercept the ball. The practice is started by one of the corner players passing to the attacking player. On receiving the pass this player can return it to the same player or pass to any of the other three, who must stay within one metre of their corner. If the defender wins the ball, it is returned to a corner player who again passes to the attacking player, and the practice continues. The players change rôles, each becoming the defender in turn.

VARIATIONS

- Do not allow the attacking player to return the ball to the player they have just received the pass from.

- Make the attacking player have three touches before passing the ball.

- Once the ball has been won by the defender, that player becomes the attacker and vice versa.

- Position two attackers and two defenders in the middle.

PASSING

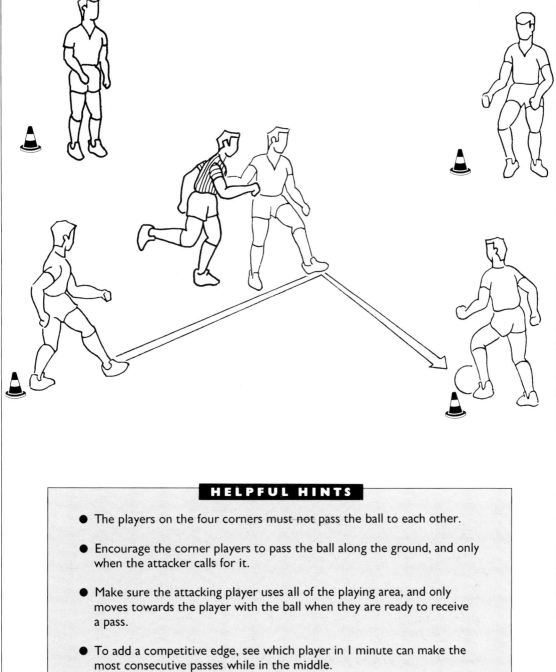

HELPFUL HINTS

● The players on the four corners must not pass the ball to each other.

● Encourage the corner players to pass the ball along the ground, and only when the attacker calls for it.

● Make sure the attacking player uses all of the playing area, and only moves towards the player with the ball when they are ready to receive a pass.

● To add a competitive edge, see which player in 1 minute can make the most consecutive passes while in the middle.

P A S S I N G

NUMBER OF PLAYERS
6 or more.

EQUIPMENT
One ball between 6 players.

PLAYING AREA
20 metres by 10 metres.

THE PRACTICE
Divide the players into groups of three. The players in each group stand behind each other in a line and the two lines of players face each other 3 metres apart. The first player in one of the lines has a ball and passes it along the ground to the player opposite. Immediately after making the pass, this player quickly turns and runs to the back of their line. The player opposite controls the pass and returns the ball before turning to join the back of their line. The practice continues with each player passing the ball and joining the back of their own line.

VARIATIONS
- Ask the players to only have one touch.
- Decrease the distance between the the two teams to only I metre.
- Ask the players to use only their weakest foot.
- Increase the distance between the two lines to I0 metres, and ask the players to pass the ball firmly.
- Ask the players to follow their pass and join the back of the line opposite.

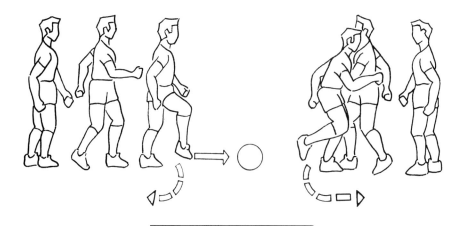

HELPFUL HINTS
- Do not have more than six players in each line.
- These passes should be made with the side of the foot.
- Make sure players turn quickly and do not stand and watch their pass.
- Encourage players to try and take just two touches – a good controlling touch and an accurate pass.

3

SHOOTING

SHOOTING

Everyone loves to score a goal and all of the following practices give players the opportunity to do just that. They range from straightforward individual practices to highly competitive but enjoyable group practices.

The Individual Practices here all encourage players to be accurate when shooting. They allow players to practise different types of shots using both feet. (Players can note the improvement in their accuracy by using a wall chart.)

The Pair Practices introduce a competitive element with players trying to score goals against each other. They require players to score through their opponent's goal or through a small goal placed between them.

The Group Practices allow players to use the skill of shooting in various competitive situations. They encourage players to find space to take shots, beat other players, to get shots in at goal and to shoot quickly and accurately when they have an opportunity. These practices do not necessarily need specialist goalkeepers but where possible, try to use them. Not only will it be of benefit to the goalkeepers but it also becomes a more realistic practice for the players.

Shooting practices are the best way to encourage players to use their weakest foot. Everyone enjoys trying themselves, and watching their team-mates' efforts.

SHOOTING

KEY COACHING POINTS FOR SHOOTING PRACTICES

No matter which part of the foot you use and what distance you shoot from, the most important point to remember when shooting is that you must always hit the target. Concentrate on making a good contact with the ball.

DRIVEN SHOTS USING THE TOP OF THE FOOT

Strike the middle of the ball, keeping the foot firm and pointing downwards with the body over the ball. Players should kick through the ball with as much power as possible without losing accuracy.

CURVED SHOTS USING THE OUTSIDE/INSIDE OF THE FOOT

Strike the side of the ball with the outside/inside part of the foot. The ankle must be firm and there must be a full follow through to achieve the curve in the shot.

PLACED SHOTS USING THE SIDE OF THE FOOT

Strike the middle of the ball with the side of the foot in the direction of the target. Side of the foot shots will help you achieve accuracy, allowing you to place the shot wherever you wish.

VOLLEYED SHOTS

Whether using the inside, outside or top of the foot, the most important points to remember are: try to get your body over the ball; strike it in the middle; do not try to hit the ball too hard.

CHIPPED SHOTS

Strike the lower half of the ball, with the foot pointing downwards. Stop the kicking action immediately after the shot. Chipped shots allow you to shoot over the goalkeeper or defending players.

Individual Practices

S H O O T I N G

BASIC SHOOTING **1**

Stand with a ball 10 metres away from and facing a wall. Gently kick the ball against the wall and control it as it returns before taking the next shot. As your accuracy improves, strike the ball more firmly.

LOW SHOOTING **2**

Mark a line half way up and across the length of the wall. Gently kick the ball, trying to hit the wall below the line and control the ball as it returns. As your shots become more accurate, strike the ball more firmly.

NUMBERED SHOOTING **3**

Divide the wall into six equal areas. Number each area. Shoot at each numbered area, controlling the ball as it returns. Concentrate on accuracy before putting more power into your shots.

V A R I A T I O N S

- Use both feet.

- Increase the distance you stand from the wall.

- As the ball returns, take just one controlling touch before attempting the next shot.

- Take shots with the ball both stationary and moving.

- Mark out the line across the wall closer to the ground or make the numbered areas smaller.

S H O O T I N G

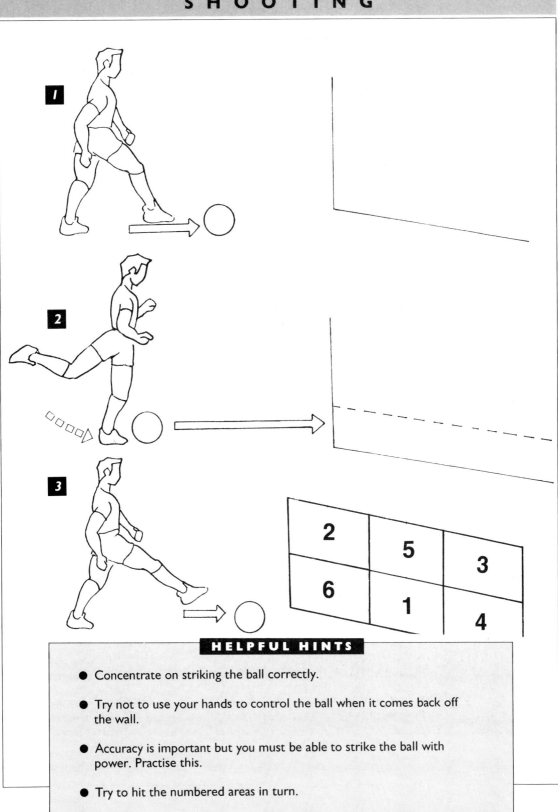

2	5	3
6	1	4

HELPFUL HINTS

● Concentrate on striking the ball correctly.

● Try not to use your hands to control the ball when it comes back off the wall.

● Accuracy is important but you must be able to strike the ball with power. Practise this.

● Try to hit the numbered areas in turn.

S H O O T I N G

SHOOTING FOR ACCURACY 1

Mark out two target areas, 1 metre square, onto a wall. Stand 10 metres away from and facing the wall with the ball at your feet. The aim of the practice is to shoot the ball to hit either of the target areas. Control the ball as it returns and repeat the practice.

TURN AND SHOOT 2

Stand 10 metres away from and with your back to the wall. Place the ball between your feet. Using the sole of your foot drag the ball back behind you. Quickly turn, move to the ball and try to hit the target areas. Control the ball as it returns and repeat the practice.

VOLLEYING AND HALF-VOLLEYING 3

Stand 10 metres away from and facing the wall with the ball in your hands. Gently drop the ball and volley or half-volley it, trying to hit the target areas. Control the ball as it returns and repeat the practice.

VARIATIONS

- Throw the ball against the wall and as it returns, without taking a controlling touch, volley or half-volley it at the target areas.

- With your back to the wall, drop the ball over the back of your head and volley or half-volley to hit the target areas.

- Gently pass the ball against the wall and hit the returning ball at the target areas.

- With your back to the wall, move the ball 1 metre out either side of you, turn and without taking a controlling touch, try to hit the target areas.

- Dribble parallel to the wall, and from a sideways-on position shoot to hit the target areas.

SHOOTING

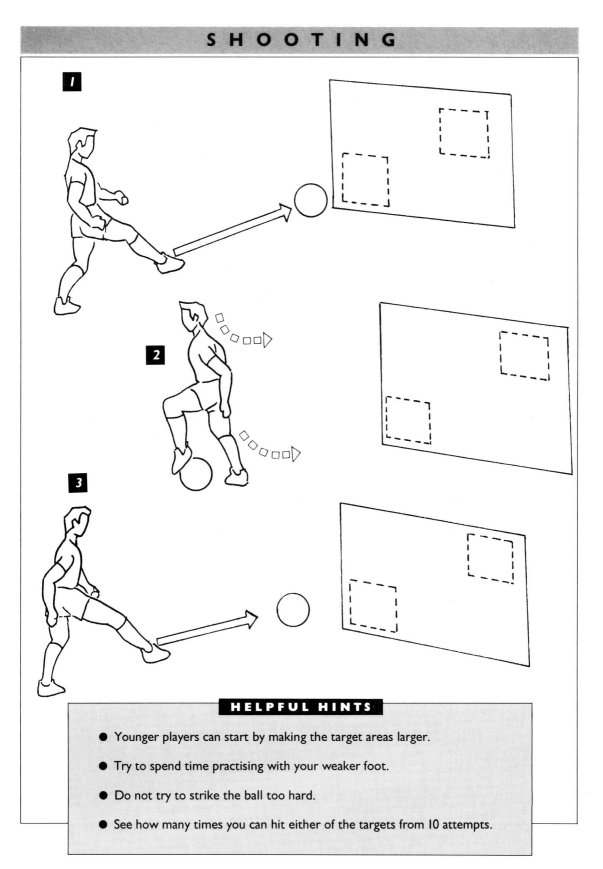

1

2

3

HELPFUL HINTS

● Younger players can start by making the target areas larger.

● Try to spend time practising with your weaker foot.

● Do not try to strike the ball too hard.

● See how many times you can hit either of the targets from 10 attempts.

Pair
Practices

SHOOTING

THE SHOOTING GAME   1

The two players stand 10 metres apart and facing each other. The object of the game is for each player to shoot the ball at their partner. Players are allowed to use their hands to control the ball and goals are awarded when shots go directly to their partner. Shots should be hit firmly.

SHOOTING FOR GOAL GAME   2

The two players stand 30 metres apart with a 3-metre wide goal between them. The object of the game is for each player to try and score. Goals are awarded when the ball has been played firmly through the goal to reach their partner opposite.

VARIATIONS

THE SHOOTING GAME
- Increase the shooting distance.

- One player acting as server lets their partner take 10 consecutive shots.

SHOOTING FOR GOAL GAME
- Try to hit the ball as hard as you can through the goal.

- Hit all of the shots along the ground.

COMBINED
- Try rolling the ball half a metre out in front of you and hit it on the move.

- Practice both these games with your weaker foot.

S H O O T I N G

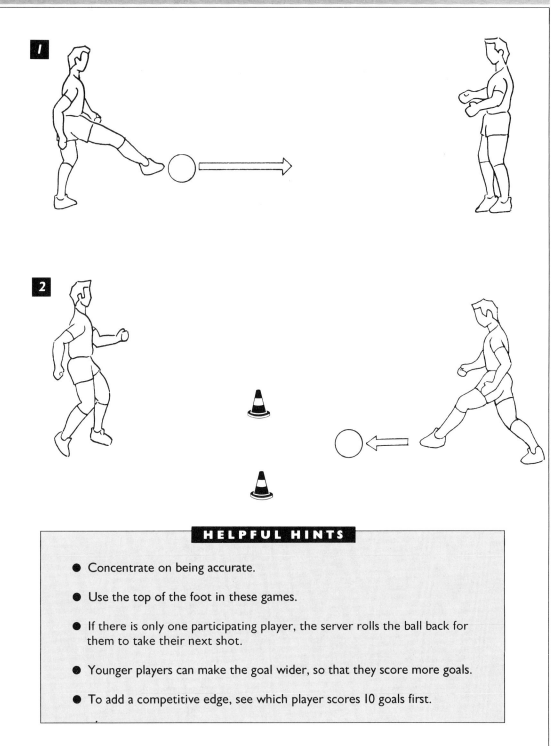

SHOOTING

VOLLEY AND SAVE 1

The two players stand 20 metres apart, each in a 5-metre wide goal. The object of the practice is for each player to try to score by volleying at their partner's goal. One of the players, with the ball in their hands, starts the practice by dropping the ball and then volleying it at their opponent's goal. The other player can stop the ball with their hands, and must move back onto the goal line before attempting their own volley. The practice continues with each player trying to score goals.

SCORING VOLLEYS 2

The two players stand 30 metres apart with a goal 2 metres wide in between them. The object of the practice is for each player to score through this goal with a volley. One player, with the ball in their hands, starts the practice by dropping the ball and then volleying it through the goal. The other player collects the shot and attempts their own volley. The practice continues with each player trying to score goals.

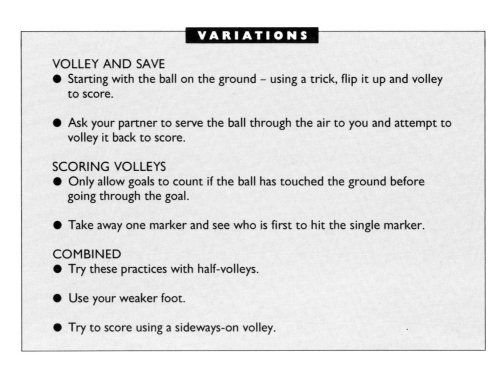

VARIATIONS

VOLLEY AND SAVE
● Starting with the ball on the ground – using a trick, flip it up and volley to score.

● Ask your partner to serve the ball through the air to you and attempt to volley it back to score.

SCORING VOLLEYS
● Only allow goals to count if the ball has touched the ground before going through the goal.

● Take away one marker and see who is first to hit the single marker.

COMBINED
● Try these practices with half-volleys.

● Use your weaker foot.

● Try to score using a sideways-on volley.

S H O O T I N G

1

2

HELPFUL HINTS

- Practise volleying into each other's hands before attempting the shooting skills.

- Younger players should start closer to the goals and concentrate on accuracy.

- Younger players can count every volley on target as a goal and the volleys that go in as three goals.

- Make these practices into competitive games by seeing who is first to score 10 goals. Only count those volleys that are under head height.

S H O O T I N G

DRIVEN SHOTS **1**

The two players stand 20 metres apart, facing each other. Half way between the players, position a 2-metre wide goal. Each player in turn hits the ball as straight and hard as they can through the goal. The ball should pass through the goal no higher than 2 metres off the ground.

'BANANA' SHOTS **2**

The two players stand 25 metres apart facing each other. In between these two players, place markers forming a goal 2 metres wide. In turn, the players try to hit the ball so that it goes around the outside of the goal to their partner. The ball can travel through the air or along the ground and should be played firmly.

VARIATIONS

DRIVEN SHOTS
- Drive the ball through the goal along the ground.

- Try these practices with your weaker foot.

- Decrease the width of the goal.

'BANANA' SHOTS
- By using the inside of both your right and left foot, try curving the ball around both sides of the goal.

- By using the outside of both your right and left foot, try curving the ball around both sides of the goal.

- Increase the width of the goal.

- Practise curving the ball at different speeds and different heights.

SHOOTING

- Allow the receiving player to use hands when controlling the ball.

- Even though you are trying to curve the ball, your aim is to shoot it accurately towards your partner's feet.

- 'Banana' shots and driven shots should be practised with both a stationary and moving ball.

- To add a competitive edge in the driven shot practice, see which player can score 10 goals first.

Group Practices

SHOOTING

NUMBER OF PLAYERS

6 or more.

EQUIPMENT

Markers and balls

PLAYING AREA

60 metres by 40 metres

THE PRACTICE

Place the goalkeepers in the goals and divide the players into equal teams. The players in each team stand behind each other in a line. Each team is positioned 40 metres from the goal they are shooting into, and towards the side of the playing area. The goalkeepers start the practice by throwing the ball to the players at the front of each line. These players dribble forward and then shoot for goal. If the shot goes wide the players retrieve the ball, return it to the goalkeeper and join the back of the other team's line. The practice continues.

VARIATIONS

- Ask the teams to start on the other side of the goal giving them the opportunity to shoot with the other foot.

- Decrease the size of the playing area and ask the players to shoot without taking a controlling touch. The goalkeepers must throw the ball out to the front players in each line at the same time.

- Ask the players to dribble around the goalkeeper before trying to score.

- Ask the two teams to start with the ball in the corners of the playing area. The first player dribbles forward and as soon as they are half-way towards the goal, the next player in the team goes.

S H O O T I N G

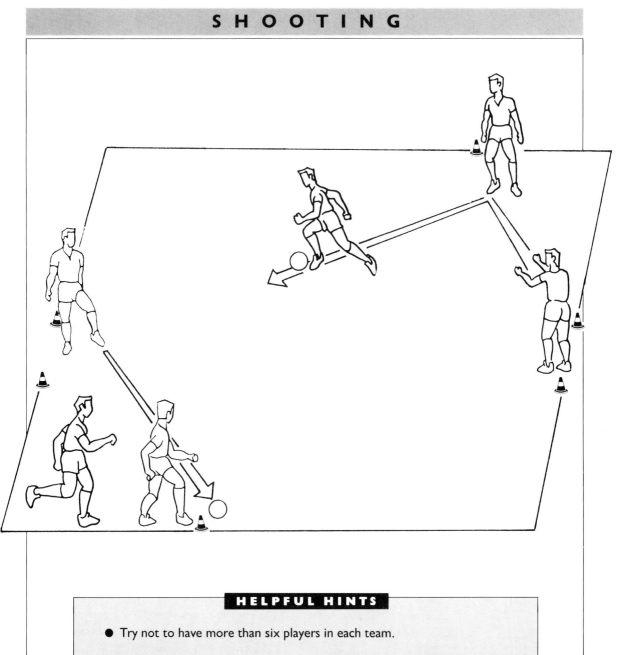

HELPFUL HINTS

- Try not to have more than six players in each team.

- The goalkeepers should serve the ball in front of the receiving players for them to run onto.

- Encourage players to stay in control of the ball and dribble quickly towards the goal.

- Try to make sure the goalkeepers serve the ball at the same time and see which player scores first.

- Make the practice competitive by seeing which player scores the most goals in a set period of time.

SHOOTING

NUMBER OF PLAYERS

3 or more.

EQUIPMENT

Markers and balls

PLAYING AREA

30 metres by 20 metres

THE PRACTICE

Divide the players into groups of three with one ball between them. Place one player in a 10-metre wide goal and on either side, 20 metres away, position the other two players. The object of the practice is for these two players to score goals. The first player shoots and if a goal is scored or the ball goes wide the player opposite retrieves the ball and takes their shot. If the 'goalkeeper' saves the ball, it is returned to either of the two players. The three players change rôles so each becomes the 'goalkeeper' in turn.

VARIATIONS

- Decrease the width of the goal.
- Only allow shots to be hit along the ground.
- Ask the 'goalkeeper' to roll the ball out to the shooting player who must shoot without taking a controlling touch.
- Ask the players to shoot with their weaker foot.

HELPFUL HINTS

- Younger players can start closer to the goal.

- Encourage players to try to be accurate and place their shots.

- When starting, make sure players are taking shots with the ball stationary.

- Make the practice competitive by seeing which player scores five goals first.

- When the players are shooting with their weaker foot, award three points for a goal, one for a shot on target and see which player reaches 10 points first.

S H O O T I N G

NUMBER OF PLAYERS

12 or more.

EQUIPMENT

Markers, balls and bibs.

PLAYING AREA

60 metres by 40 metres.

THE PRACTICE

Place the goalkeepers in the goals and divide the rest of the players into two equal teams. Four players in each team are restricted to the defending half of the pitch while the other two are restricted to the attacking half. The object of the practice is for both teams to have as many shots as possible. The players, while keeping to their restricted halves, can pass the ball to each other to try to get into a better shooting position. If a goal is scored, or the ball goes over the goal-line, the goalkeeper re-starts the game by rolling it back in. If it goes out over the side-line, the team whose possession it is must roll the ball back in.

VARIATIONS

- The four players restricted to the defending half must play either one touch or two touch.
- Players are only allowed to shoot from the defending half after a pass has been played across the half-way line and received back.
- All passes and shots must be played below head height.
- Allow one of the four defending players to go over the half-way line.
- Try this practice without using goalkeepers.

HELPFUL HINTS

- For younger players, shorten the length of the playing area, so that the players can have shots at goal from deep in their own half.
- Encourage the players in the attacking half to follow in all shots in case of goalkeeping error.
- Always ensure the defending players outnumber the attacking players in each half of the playing area.
- The goalkeepers should only be allowed to throw the ball out to the players in the defending half.

S H O O T I N G

NUMBER OF PLAYERS
8 or more.

EQUIPMENT
Markers, bibs and balls

PLAYING AREA
40 metres by 25 metres

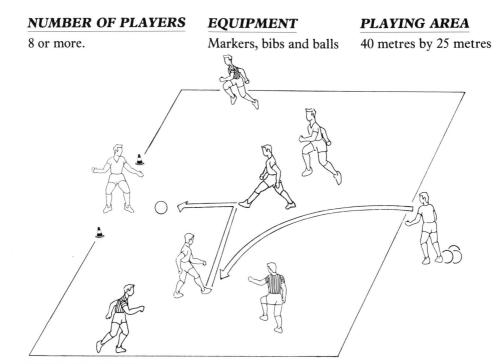

THE PRACTICE

Position the goalkeeper in the goal and divide the players into two equal teams. The server starts the practice by passing the ball anywhere into the playing area. The object of this practice is for each team to gain possession in order to shoot at the goal. The team in possession can pass the ball to each other and use the server who joins in to become an extra player in their team. The server cannot shoot or enter the playing area. All the players must stay inside the playing area and when the ball goes out the server passes another ball in. The practice continues for a set period of time.

VARIATIONS

- Try the practice with each player given an opposing player to mark.
- Allow the serving player to enter the playing area, but again do not allow them to shoot.
- Only allow the players in the team to shoot after they have made three or more consecutive passes.
- Allow the serving player to shoot from outside the playing area.

HELPFUL HINTS

- The serving player should move across the whole width of the playing area to help the team in possession.
- Try not to have more than three players in each team.
- If you have a large number of players, divide them into groups of three, with the resting players retrieving the balls and returning them to the server.
- The first team to score three goals stays in the playing area and plays the next team.

S H O O T I N G

NUMBER OF PLAYERS
6 or more.

EQUIPMENT
3 balls and markers.

PLAYING AREA
40 metres by 25 metres.

THE PRACTICE

Place a goalkeeper in the goal with the other players in a line, 30 metres away from and facing the goal. One player is positioned half-way between the goal and the line of players. The first player in the line passes the ball into this player who, with one touch, sets the ball to either side for the shooting player to try to score with a first time shot. The practice continues with each player taking a shot, retrieving their ball and joining the back of the line.

VARIATIONS

- Make players call out which side they want the returning pass to be played.
- Allow the player in the middle to pick the ball up, or flick the ball into the air, making the shooting player volley or half-volley.
- Allow the shooting player two touches, one to control and the next to shoot.
- Ask the middle player to set the ball out wider.
- Play two passes with the middle player before taking the shot.

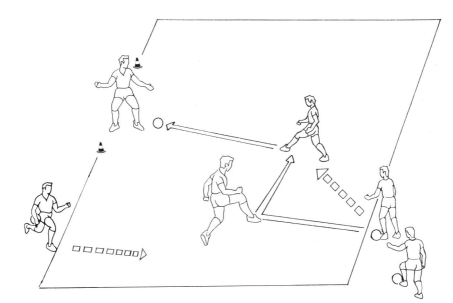

HELPFUL HINTS

- With younger players, make the shooting distance shorter.
- Change the middle player after a period of time.
- To increase the number of shots players have in the session, make sure the next player in the line is ready to go.
- To add competition to this practice, award points – one for a shot on target, three for a goal – and see which player scores 10 points first.

S H O O T I N G

NUMBER OF PLAYERS

6 or more.

EQUIPMENT

3 balls and markers.

PLAYING AREA

40 metres by 25 metres.

THE PRACTICE

The players are divided into two teams. The players in each team stand behind each other in a line. One team stands behind a marker facing the goal on the left hand side of the playing area, and the other team stand behind a marker placed on the right hand side of the area. The team of players on the left have a ball each. The first player in the line passes the ball along the ground in front of the on-coming player from the other team. This player shoots for goal immediately without a controlling touch. The passing player joins the end of the other team's line while the shooting player follows the shot and retrieves the ball. This player joins the back of the serving line and the practice continues.

VARIATIONS

● The shooting players are allowed one touch to control before taking their shots.

● Increase and decrease the distance of the serving pass.

● Change the angle of the serving pass.

● The shooting and passing lines change sides.

● One player is positioned permanently 10 metres in front of the goalkeeper and is allowed to follow in after every shot in case the keeper does not gather the ball safely.

SHOOTING

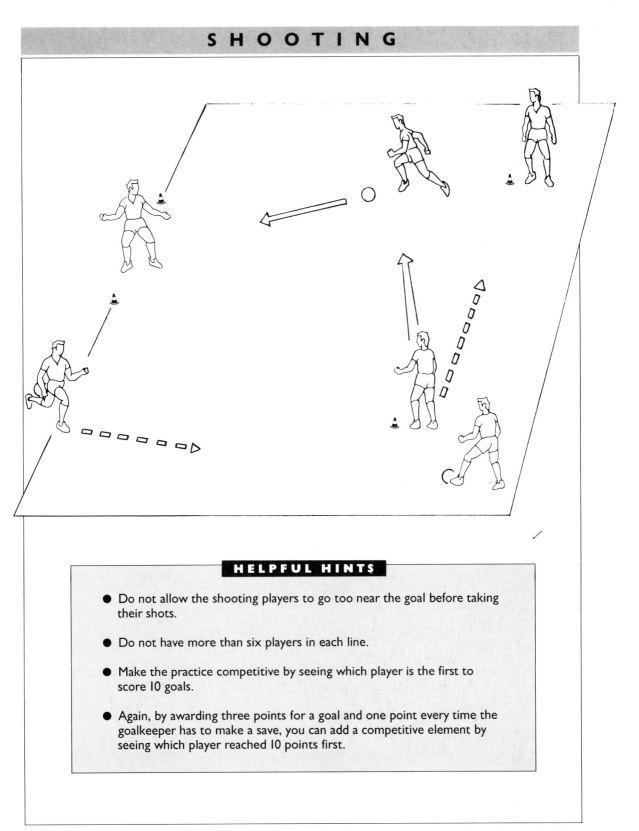

HELPFUL HINTS

- Do not allow the shooting players to go too near the goal before taking their shots.

- Do not have more than six players in each line.

- Make the practice competitive by seeing which player is the first to score 10 goals.

- Again, by awarding three points for a goal and one point every time the goalkeeper has to make a save, you can add a competitive element by seeing which player reached 10 points first.

SHOOTING

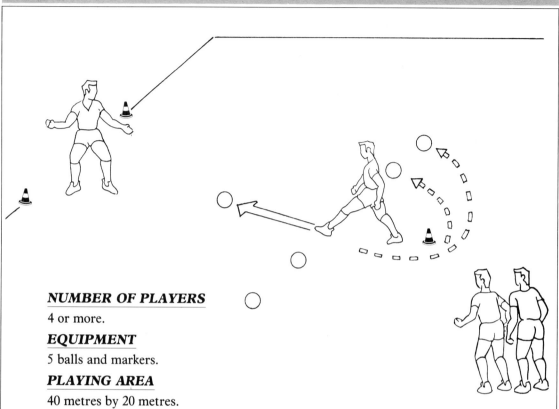

NUMBER OF PLAYERS

4 or more.

EQUIPMENT

5 balls and markers.

PLAYING AREA

40 metres by 20 metres.

THE PRACTICE

Place a goalkeeper in the goal. Position five balls outside the playing area, side by side, 1 metre apart. The object of this practice is for the shooting player to try to score with each ball. After every shot the player turns and runs around a marker, which is positioned 5 metres behind the balls. The practice finishes when all five shots have been taken and the next player takes a turn. The other players in the group stand behind the goal and retrieve the balls.

VARIATIONS

- Ask the players to take their shots without running around the marker each time.
- Keep retrieving the balls and work the shooting player for one minute.
- Allow the players to have one touch before shooting.
- Place the marker between the balls and the goal.
- Spread the balls along the full width of the playing area.

HELPFUL HINTS

- For younger players, position the balls closer to the goal.
- Do not allow players to use only their strongest foot.
- Encourage players to make their sprints and turns as quickly as possible.
- Ask players to try and be aware of the goalkeeper's position before taking their shots.
- See how many goals each player scores in one minute.

S H O O T I N G

NUMBER OF PLAYERS
6 or more.

EQUIPMENT
Markers and balls.

PLAYING AREA
40 metres by 30 metres.

THE PRACTICE

Place the goalkeeper in the goal and divide the players into pairs. One of each pair stands behind a marker on the touchline, and their partner, who has the ball, stands in line with and facing the goal, which is 40 metres away. The player in possession passes to their partner, who dribbles quickly down the touchline before crossing the ball for them to take a first-time shot. As soon as the shot is taken, the next pair go and the practice continues.

VARIATIONS

- Place a defender in front of the goalkeeper and add an extra attacking player.
- Place two defenders in front of the goalkeeper and add two extra attacking players.
- Allow the player shooting to have one controlling touch before taking a shot.
- Ask the wide player to dribble the full length of the playing area before crossing.
- Ask the wide player to start on the other side of the playing area.

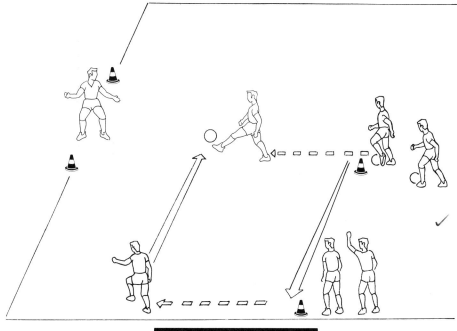

HELPFUL HINTS

- The player who has just taken the shot must retrieve the ball and return back to the start, keeping off the playing area.
- Alternate each pair to ensure that both players have the opportunity to cross and shoot.
- Goalkeepers must stay within 5 metres of their line.
- Make the practice competitive by seeing which pair score the most goals from 10 attempts.

SHOOTING

NUMBER OF PLAYERS

8 or more.

EQUIPMENT

One ball, markers and bibs.

PLAYING AREA

40 metres by 30 metres.

THE PRACTICE

Divide the players into two equal teams and place the goalkeepers in the goals. The object of this practice is to encourage all the outfield players of both teams to shoot at their opponents' goal as often as possible. The players are allowed to dribble the ball and pass to each other before attempting shots. After a goal is scored or the ball is retrieved from behind the goal, the goalkeeper restarts the practice by rolling it to an available team mate. If the ball goes out of the sides of the playing area the game is restarted with the player whose possession it now is rolling it back in.

VARIATIONS

- By placing two markers on the goal-line, 1 metre apart, and not using goalkeepers, the players are awarded three goals if they score through the markers and one in the full size goal.
- Allow the players only two touches – one to control and the next to pass or shoot.
- Only allow players to shoot after their team has made at least three consecutive passes.
- Do not allow the ball to go above head height.

HELPFUL HINTS

- For younger players, shorten the length of the pitch.
- Keep a supply of balls in the goals so that the practice is continuous.
- Goalkeepers must stay within 5 metres of their line.
- Make the practice competitive by either playing for a period of 10 minutes to see which team scores the most goals or by seeing which team scores 10 goals first.

S H O O T I N G

NUMBER OF PLAYERS

6 or more.

EQUIPMENT

Markers and balls.

PLAYING AREA

20 metres by 20 metres.

THE PRACTICE

Place a goalkeeper in the goal, and divide the rest of the players into pairs. The first pair stand 20 metres away, facing the goal. With both players looking directly towards the goal, the server, standing behind them, throws or rolls the ball between them. As the players see the ball they must try to shoot as quickly as possible, as they are competing against each other for the chance to score. The practice continues with pairs of players trying to score.

VARIATIONS

- Ask the players to face away from the goal, and position the server between them and the goal.
- Serve the ball at different heights.
- Increase the distance between the players and the goal.
- Start the pairs on either the right or left side of the playing area.
- Allow the player who reaches the ball first to try and dribble around the goalkeeper.

HELPFUL HINTS

- Change the pairings around so that the players all play against each other.

- Make sure the players cannot see the ball being served.

- Encourage both players to be competitive, so that if they are not making a shot, they are trying to stop their partner.

- By awarding one point for a shot and three for a goal, see which player scores 10 points first.

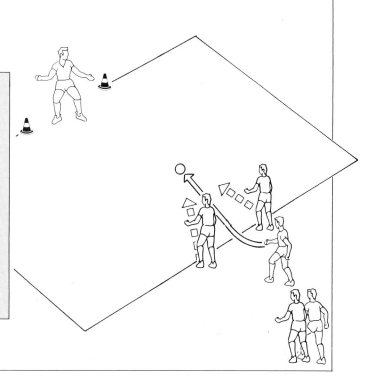

SHOOTING

NUMBER OF PLAYERS
8 or more.

EQUIPMENT
Markers and balls.

PLAYING AREA
30 metres by 25 metres.

THE PRACTICE
Divide the players into two teams of three and position a goalkeeper in the goal. The server starts the practice by throwing the ball anywhere into the playing area. The object of the practice is for both teams to try to score goals. As soon as a goal is scored, or the ball goes out of the playing area, the server throws another ball in. The practice continues for a set period of time.

VARIATIONS
- Only allow players two touches; one to control, the other to shoot or pass.
- Players can only have a shot if they have first made a pass to a player in their team.
- Introduce the offside rule into this practice.
- Decrease the size of the playing area.

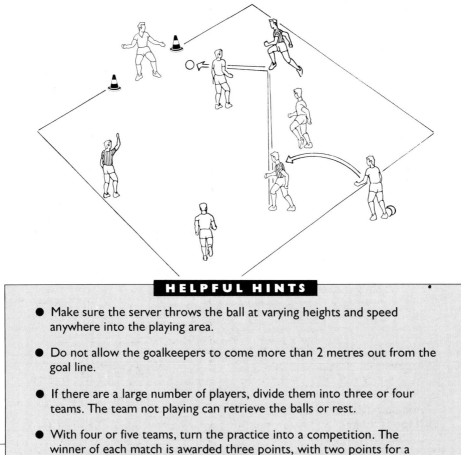

HELPFUL HINTS
- Make sure the server throws the ball at varying heights and speed anywhere into the playing area.

- Do not allow the goalkeepers to come more than 2 metres out from the goal line.

- If there are a large number of players, divide them into three or four teams. The team not playing can retrieve the balls or rest.

- With four or five teams, turn the practice into a competition. The winner of each match is awarded three points, with two points for a draw and one for a defeat. An extra point is given for each goal scored.

S H O O T I N G

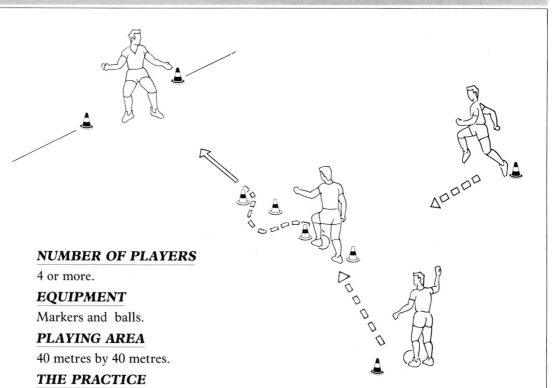

NUMBER OF PLAYERS

4 or more.

EQUIPMENT

Markers and balls.

PLAYING AREA

40 metres by 40 metres.

THE PRACTICE

Place a goalkeeper in the goal and divide the rest of the players into pairs, one as an attacker and the other as a defender. Both players start from a point 5 metres away from the four markers that are in line with the goal. The object of the practice is for the attacking player to dribble the ball around the four markers before shooting at goal. The defender who also has to run in and out of the markers, can only start when the attacking playing has reached the second marker. After the shot or interception, the pair join the back of the group, change rôles, and the next pair go.

VARIATIONS

- Only allow the attackers two touches once they have passed the final marker
- Increase the distance between the markers.
- Add two more markers.
- Allow the attacking players to dribble around the goalkeeper.
- Allow the defending players to try to win the ball without having to run in and out of the markers.

HELPFUL HINTS

- For younger players, only have two markers and allow the defending player to set off when the attacker has reached the first marker.
- Goalkeepers should not move off their line until the attacking player has rounded the last marker.
- If the attacking players are not getting enough shots, adjust the starting position of the defenders
- Make the practice competitive by seeing which player scores 10 goals first.

SHOOTING

NUMBER OF PLAYERS

6 or more.

EQUIPMENT

Markers and balls.

PLAYING AREA

30 metres by 20 metres.

THE PRACTICE

Place the goalkeeper in the goal and position the rest of the players inside the playing area. The server, who is outside the area and facing the goal, throws the ball anywhere into the playing area. The object of this game is for all the players to play against each other, trying to score goals. They must stay in the playing area, and when the ball goes out or a goal is scored, the server throws another ball in.

VARIATIONS

- Only allow the players one touch.
- Serve two balls in at the same time.
- Also award a goal if a player passes the ball back to the server.
- When a player scores a goal, allow them to come out of the playing area, and see which player is the last one left in.

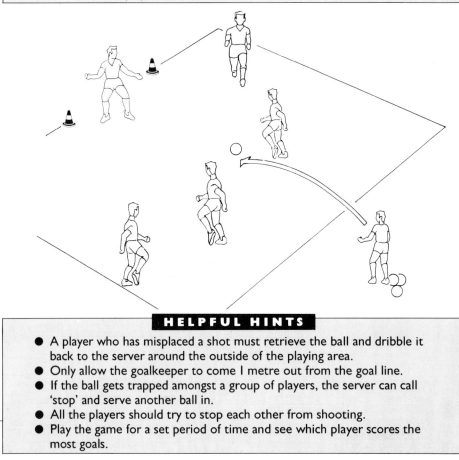

HELPFUL HINTS

- A player who has misplaced a shot must retrieve the ball and dribble it back to the server around the outside of the playing area.
- Only allow the goalkeeper to come 1 metre out from the goal line.
- If the ball gets trapped amongst a group of players, the server can call 'stop' and serve another ball in.
- All the players should try to stop each other from shooting.
- Play the game for a set period of time and see which player scores the most goals.

4

HEADING

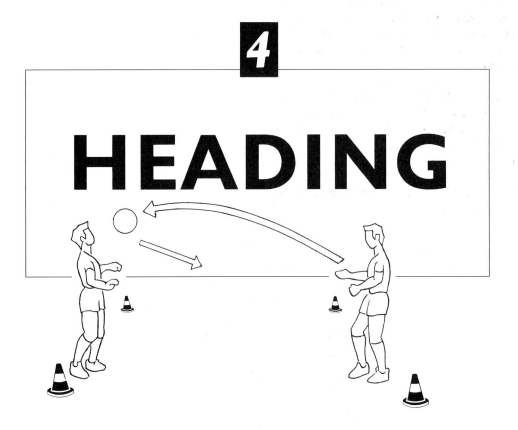

HEADING

Although heading is the least natural skill, and the least used, players should spend time practising it. The practices that follow cover a wide variety of heading skills and are, in the main, non-competitive.

Players should start with the simple practices and only attempt the more demanding ones when they are heading the ball correctly. Young players should avoid doing heading practices for long periods.

The Individual Practices can be done in any open space or against a wall. Young players can easily chart their progress by seeing how many consecutive headers they can make.

The Pair Practices can involve another player or simply a server. Each of the practices have variations and all provide a competitive edge without physical contact.

The Group Practices include all the heading skills previously practised by individuals and pairs.

HEADING

KEY COACHING POINTS FOR HEADING PRACTICES

The main points to remember when practising heading are for players to move into the line of the oncoming ball, watch it carefully and make a good contact on the ball with their forehead.

ATTACKING HEADING

Watch the ball carefully and concentrate on accuracy before power. The most important point to remember is to head the ball down. Players can make these headers from either a standing position or by jumping into the air.

DEFENSIVE HEADING

Watch the ball carefully and concentrate on heading the ball as far and high as possible. The power for this header comes from the forward movement of the whole of the top half of the body as the forehead makes contact with the ball. These headers can be made from a standing position or by jumping into the air.

GLANCING HEADERS

Unlike the majority of headers made, glancing headers use the side or top of the forehead and do not require a firm contact with the ball. This header allows players to slightly change the direction in which the ball is travelling – glancing it to either side or upwards and downwards.

Individual Practices

HEADING

BASIC HEADING   **1**

Stand 5 metres away from and facing the wall. Throw the ball against the wall so that it comes back to you at head height. Head the ball firmly against the wall and catch it as it returns.

DOWNWARD HEADING   **2**

Stand 5 metres away from and facing the wall. Mark a line half-way up across the wall. Throw the ball against the wall so that it comes back to you at head height. Head the ball to try to hit the wall below the line.

HEADING FOR ACCURACY   **3**

Mark out six equal areas on the wall. Number each area. Throw the ball against the wall so that it comes back to you at head height. Try to head the ball into the numbered areas.

VARIATIONS

- Standing close to the wall, see how many consecutive headers you can make against it.

- Vary the height and speed of the service against the wall.

- Serve the ball against the wall, so that you have to jump to head the returning ball.

- Serve the ball against the wall, then turn completely around before you head the returning ball.

H E A D I N G

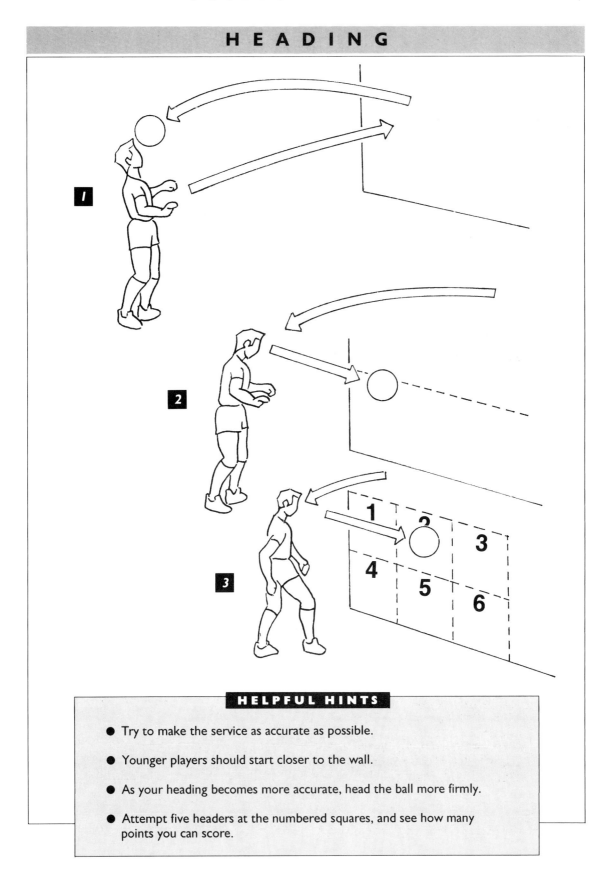

HELPFUL HINTS

● Try to make the service as accurate as possible.

● Younger players should start closer to the wall.

● As your heading becomes more accurate, head the ball more firmly.

● Attempt five headers at the numbered squares, and see how many points you can score.

HEADING

STAND AND HEAD █ 1

Standing still, throw the ball 1 metre into the air above your head. As it drops, head the ball straight back up. The header should reach the height of your throw, and drop back into your hands.

JUMP AND HEAD ■ 2

Throw the ball 2 metres into the air above your head. As it drops, jump into the air and head the ball straight back up. The header should go higher than your throw, and drop back into your hands.

RUN AND HEAD ■ 3

Throw the ball 1 metre into the air above your head and just out in front of you. Move forward to head the ball as it drops back down. The header should go slightly forward and no more than 1 metre into the air. Continue moving forward, heading and catching the ball.

■ VARIATIONS

- Try to vary the height of your headers, from gently controlled efforts to high, powerful ones.

- Throw the ball higher into the air.

- When jumping to head, practise jumping into the air off one foot, and then practise two-footed take-offs.

- While sitting on the ground, throw the ball into the air and try to make consecutive headers.

- While sitting, throw the ball into the air, head it firmly and try to stand up and catch the ball before it hits the ground.

H E A D I N G

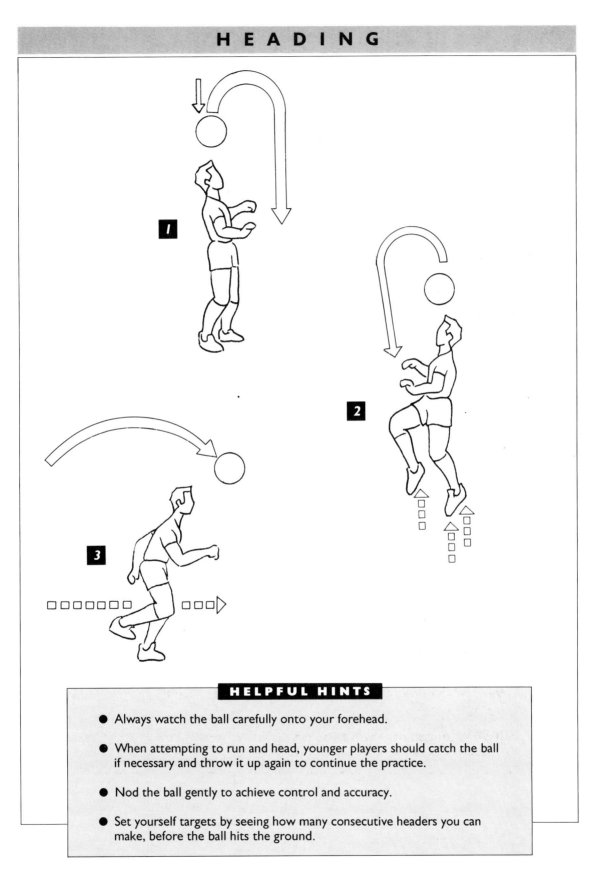

HELPFUL HINTS

● Always watch the ball carefully onto your forehead.

● When attempting to run and head, younger players should catch the ball if necessary and throw it up again to continue the practice.

● Nod the ball gently to achieve control and accuracy.

● Set yourself targets by seeing how many consecutive headers you can make, before the ball hits the ground.

H E A D I N G

STATIONARY HEADERS **I**

Stand 10 metres away from and facing the wall. Throw the ball into the air, and as it drops head it at the wall. Collect the ball and repeat the practice.

RUNNING HEADERS **2**

Stand 10 metres away from and facing the wall. Throw the ball into the air out in front of you. Run forwards and head the ball at the wall. Collect the ball and repeat the practice.

RUNNING AND JUMPING HEADERS **3**

Stand 10 metres away from and facing the wall. Throw the ball into the air out in front of you. Run forward and jump to head the ball at the wall. Collect the ball and repeat the practice.

V A R I A T I O N S

- Try to head the ball higher up the wall.

- Head the ball firmly towards the bottom of the wall.

- Throw the ball into the air, and let it bounce and then head the ball at the wall.

- Stand sideways-on to the wall, throw the ball into the air and head it against the wall.

H E A D I N G

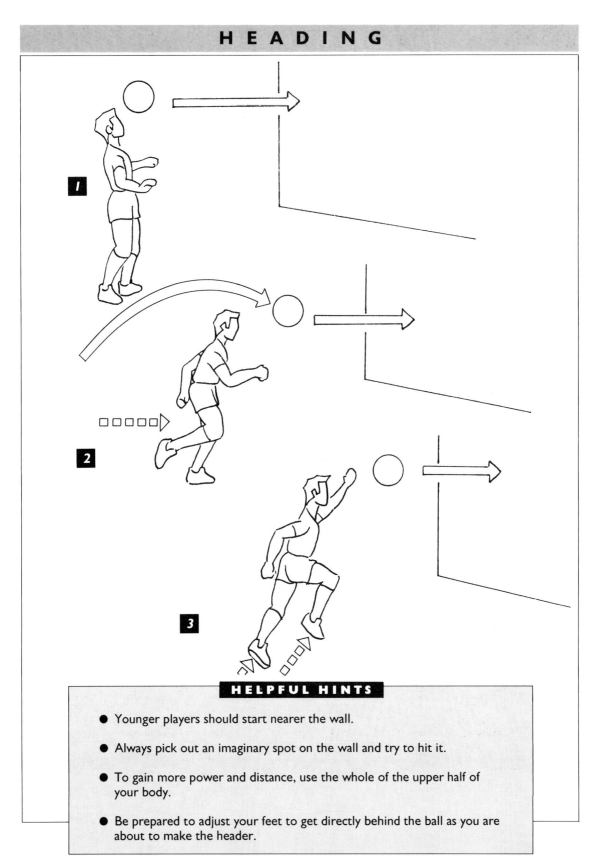

HELPFUL HINTS

● Younger players should start nearer the wall.

● Always pick out an imaginary spot on the wall and try to hit it.

● To gain more power and distance, use the whole of the upper half of your body.

● Be prepared to adjust your feet to get directly behind the ball as you are about to make the header.

Pair Practices

HEADING

HEADING FOR GOAL **1**

Mark out two goals 3 metres wide and 10 metres apart. Each player stands in a goal. The object of the game is for the serving player to throw the ball into the air for the other player to try and head it back past them to score. One player acts as the server and goalkeeper and after 10 consecutive serves the players change roles.

POWER HEADING FOR GOAL **2**

Mark out two goals, 2 metres wide and 10 metres apart. Each player stands in a goal. In turn they throw the ball into the air slightly in front of them and try to head it into their partner's goal. The practice continues.

VARIATIONS

HEADING FOR GOAL
- Serve the ball for the working player to jump into the air to head it back.

- Players must have a controlling header before heading for goal.

- Goals can only be scored below waist height.

POWER HEADING FOR GOAL
- Players must be off the ground when heading for goal.

- Stand sideways on, throw the ball into the air and head for goal.

COMBINED
- Players who are defending the goals cannot use their hands.

H E A D I N G

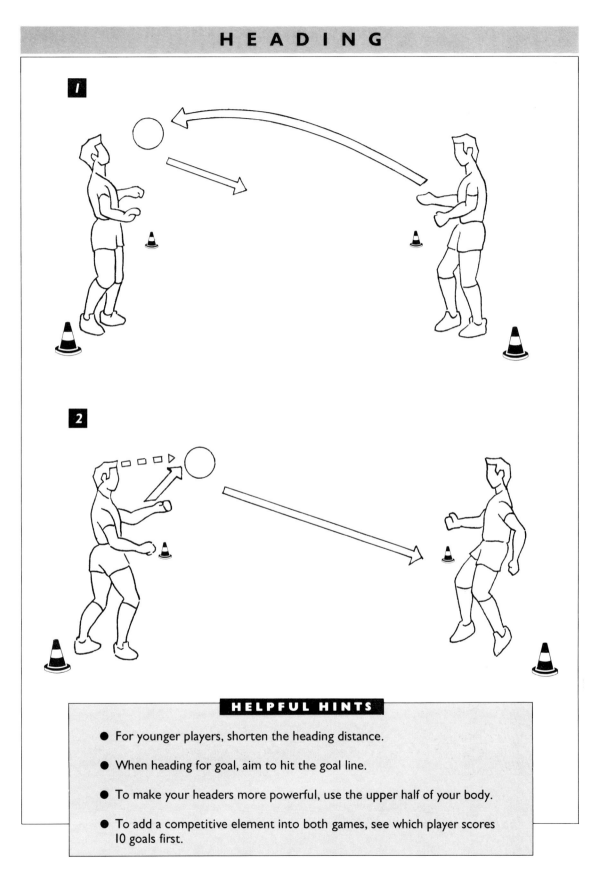

HELPFUL HINTS

● For younger players, shorten the heading distance.

● When heading for goal, aim to hit the goal line.

● To make your headers more powerful, use the upper half of your body.

● To add a competitive element into both games, see which player scores 10 goals first.

H E A D I N G

CONTROLLED HEADING **1**

The two players stand facing each other 5 metres apart. One player throws the ball gently towards their partner who makes a controlling header and then continues to keep the ball in the air with their head. The object is to make as many headers as possible before losing control. Once control is lost, the players change rôles.

CONTINUOUS HEADING GAME **2**

The two players stand facing each other 5 metres apart. The object of this game is for the players to keep heading the ball backwards and forwards to each other without losing control. No other part of the body can be used to control the ball.

VARIATIONS

CONTROLLED HEADING
● Make alternate low and high headers whilst keeping the ball up.

● Move forward 10 paces, keeping the ball up, and then move back to the start.

CONTINUOUS HEADING
● Each player must head the ball twice before returning the header.

● Whilst keeping the ball up, see how far you can both travel before losing control of the ball.

● Stand 1 metre apart and see how many consecutive headers you can make.

HELPFUL HINTS

● Younger players can catch the ball in order to keep the continuous game going.

● When trying to make consecutive headers on your own, don't head the ball too far into the air.

● These are very difficult skills – don't expect too much too early.

● Make the practices more competitive by seeing which player makes the most consecutive headers. Now see how many consecutive headers you make between you.

H E A D I N G

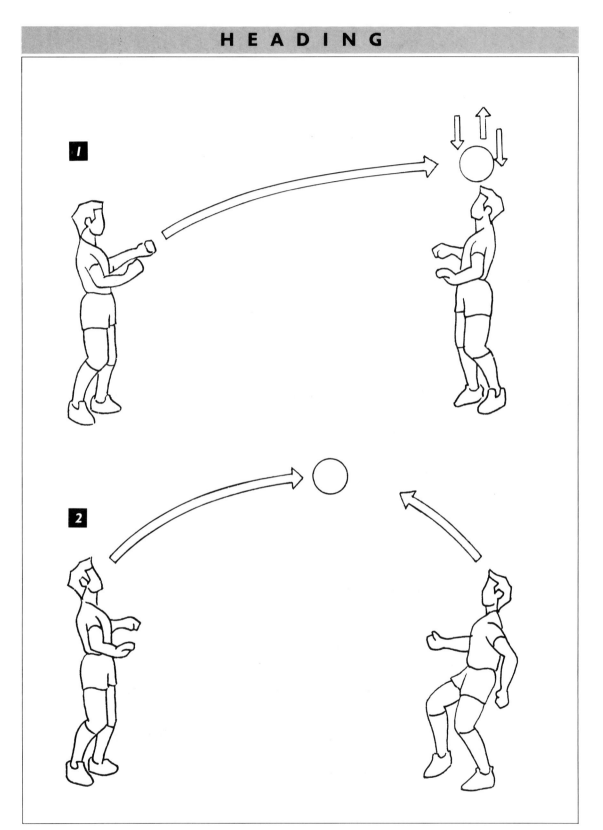

HEADING

ATTACKING HEADING   1

The two players stand facing each other, 10 metres apart. The server throws the ball to the working player who heads the ball back towards the feet of the server. The practice continues with the players changing rôles after a set period of time or number of headers.

DEFENSIVE HEADING   2

The two players stand facing each other 10 metres apart. The server throws the ball to the working player who heads the ball as far over the top of the serving player as possible. The practice continues with the players changing roles after a set period of time or number of headers.

VARIATIONS

ATTACKING HEADING
- Make the server bounce the ball mid-way between the two players.

- Serve the ball more quickly towards the working player.

- Serve the ball in front of the working player, making them dive forward to head the ball.

DEFENSIVE HEADING
- Make the server throw the ball at least 15 metres into the air.

- Serve the ball over the working player's head, making them move backwards before heading the ball.

COMBINED
- Make the working player stand facing away from the server and then, when the server calls, turn to head the ball back.

- Ask the working player to be moving forward and jump to meet the service.

- Serve the ball to the side of the working player, making them move to head the ball.

H E A D I N G

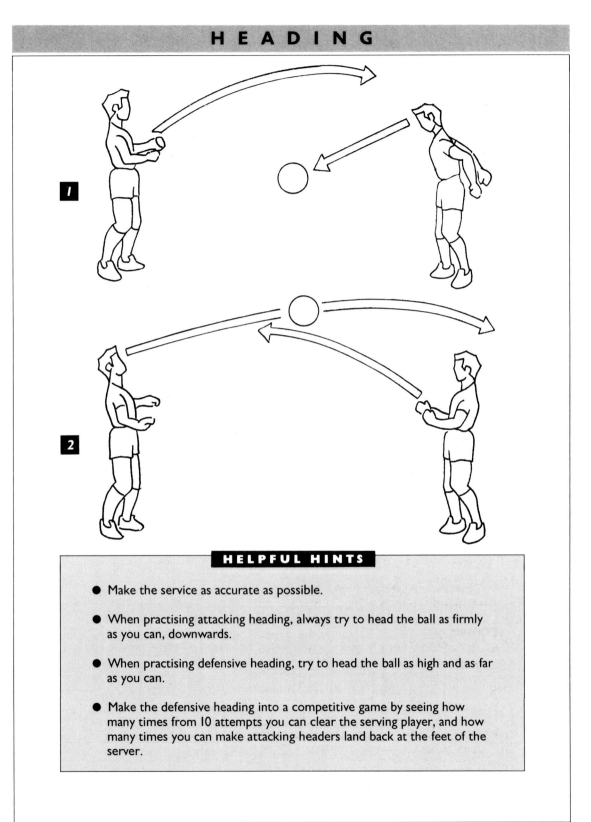

HELPFUL HINTS

● Make the service as accurate as possible.

● When practising attacking heading, always try to head the ball as firmly as you can, downwards.

● When practising defensive heading, try to head the ball as high and as far as you can.

● Make the defensive heading into a competitive game by seeing how many times from 10 attempts you can clear the serving player, and how many times you can make attacking headers land back at the feet of the server.

Group Practices

HEADING

NUMBER OF PLAYERS
5 or more.

EQUIPMENT
Four balls and markers.

PLAYING AREA
20 metres by 20 metres.

THE PRACTICE
Four players stand on each corner of a 20 metres by 20 metres area. Each of these players has a ball. The fifth player is positioned in the middle and receives serves, in any order, from the four outside players, the object of the practice being to see how many headers the middle player can make in one minute. The headers must go back to the server without touching the ground and the middle player must receive a serve from a different player each time. Each player takes a turn in the middle.

VARIATIONS

- Make the middle player jump in the air to head the ball.

- Make the player have one controlling header before heading the ball back.

- Serve the ball to make the middle player move closer towards the servers to head the ball.

- Only have three serving players with a ball and ask the middle player to head the ball to the player not in possession of a ball.

- Try this practice with three players, one in the middle and the other two on either side with a ball.

H E A D I N G

HELPFUL HINTS

- For younger players, make the playing area smaller.

- Do not introduce the competitive element into the practice until the players are heading the ball accurately.

- Ask the middle player to call for the ball.

- Do not count a header as successful if the outside players have to move off the markers to catch the ball.

HEADING

NUMBER OF PLAYERS
7 or more.

EQUIPMENT
Markers and balls.

PLAYING AREA
30 metres by 25 metres.

THE PRACTICE
Place the goalkeeper in goal and divide the players into two equal teams. The players in each team stand behind each other in a line 15 metres away from the goal and 10 metres apart from the other team. One team is in possession of the balls. The first player in this team throws a ball into the air just in front of the first player in the other team for them to head at goal. The server goes to the back of the line of the team who are heading, and the player who has just headed at goal retrieves the ball and joins the back of the serving team. The practice continues.

VARIATIONS

● Move the serving team closer to the goal to change the angle of the service.

● Serve the ball more firmly at waist height, and ask the players to try diving headers.

● Ask the heading line to change rôles and serve the ball.

● Increase the distance between the two teams, and ask the players to serve the ball with a volley or a chipped pass.

H E A D I N G

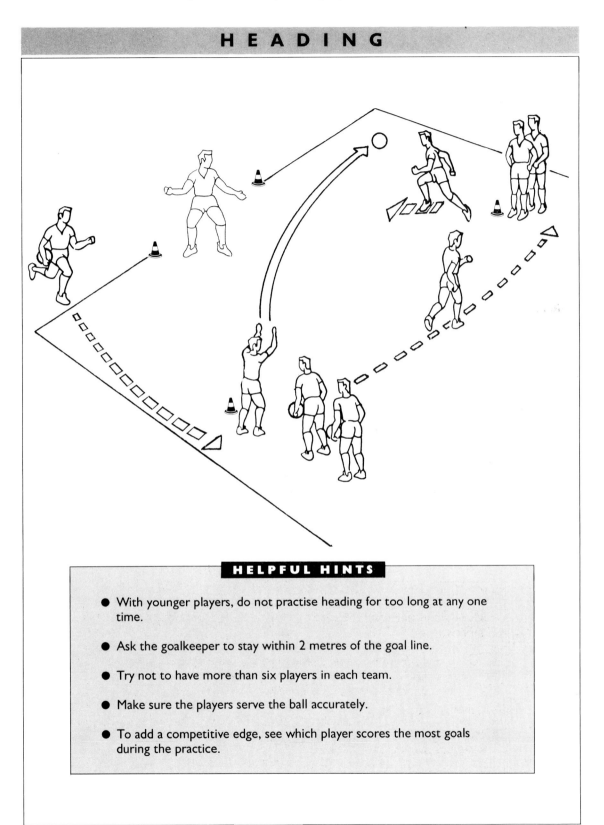

HELPFUL HINTS

- With younger players, do not practise heading for too long at any one time.

- Ask the goalkeeper to stay within 2 metres of the goal line.

- Try not to have more than six players in each team.

- Make sure the players serve the ball accurately.

- To add a competitive edge, see which player scores the most goals during the practice.

HEADING

NUMBER OF PLAYERS

8 or more.

EQUIPMENT

One ball, markers and bibs.

PLAYING AREA

40 metres by 30 metres.

THE PRACTICE

The players are divided into two equal teams. The players in each team pass the ball between themselves by first throwing the ball, then heading it, before being able to catch it again. The object of this game is for each team to try to score through 3-metre wide goals with headers only. Teams can make consecutive headers but must always head the ball after a throw. The defending team tries to intercept the ball – they can only head it after an opposing player has thrown it, but can catch or head the ball after a header. If the ball goes out of the playing area it is thrown back in. Play for a set period of time or until one team scores 10 goals.

VARIATIONS

● Play this game without goalkeepers.

● Do not allow players to throw the ball any further than 5 metres.

● Only allow players to score if they are within 3 metres of the goal line.

● Make the goals bigger.

● Do not allow players to head the ball back to the player who has just thrown it to them.

H E A D I N G

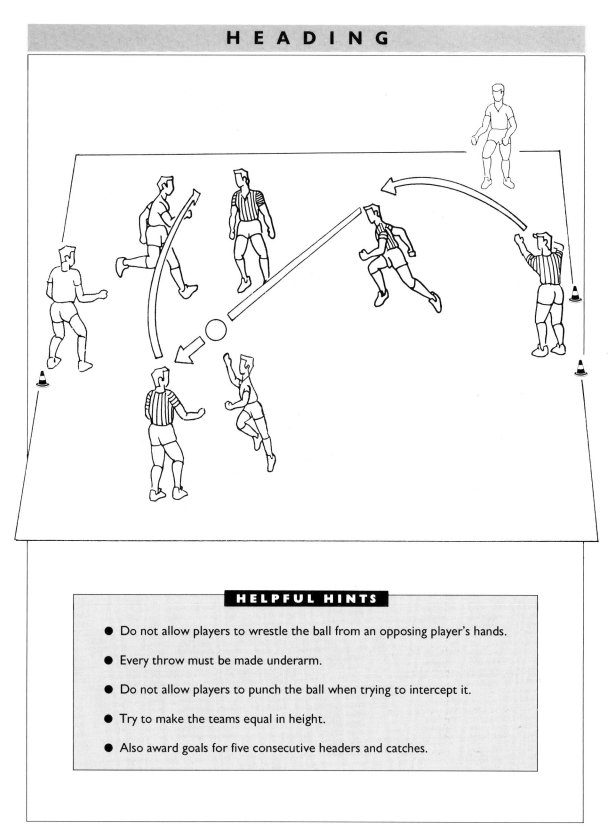

HELPFUL HINTS

● Do not allow players to wrestle the ball from an opposing player's hands.

● Every throw must be made underarm.

● Do not allow players to punch the ball when trying to intercept it.

● Try to make the teams equal in height.

● Also award goals for five consecutive headers and catches.

H E A D I N G

NUMBER OF PLAYERS
5 or more.

EQUIPMENT
One ball for each group.

PLAYING AREA
10 metres by 10 metres.

THE PRACTICE

The group of players, with one ball between them, form a circle. One player stands in the middle. The object of this practice is for the players to keep the ball off the ground by heading the ball to each other. The practice is started by the middle player throwing the ball to any other player who heads it back to the middle player. From this point on the ball must only be headed, with the middle player heading the ball to any of the players forming the circle. If the ball hits the ground, the practice is re-started by the player in the middle.

VARIATIONS

- Allow the middle player a controlling header before heading to the next player.
- Allow the players forming the circle to head to each other as well as the player in the middle.
- Make the circle smaller and ask the middle player to go quickly around the circle serving the ball and catching the returning header.
- Ask the middle player to go around the circle making headers in turn with each of the players forming the circle.

HELPFUL HINTS

- With younger players, allow the middle player to catch the ball to keep the practice going.

- Do not have more than seven players forming a circle. If you do have a large number of players, form more than one circle.

- Encourage players to stay on their toes so they can quickly adjust their position to head the ball.

- To add a competitive edge see which middle player makes the most consecutive headers with the players forming a circle.

5

SMALL SIDED GAMES

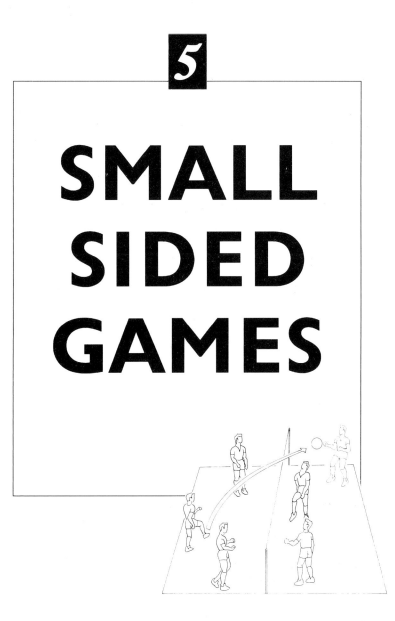

SMALL-SIDED GAMES

The following small-sided games allow players to put into practice the skills they have been working on. Players benefit from these because they provide the opportunity for them to have lots of touches of the ball whilst in direct competition with opposing players.

These games encourage teamwork and understanding between players. They make them aware of the need to keep thinking and moving in order to help their team. They allow players to work out how to find space in which to play or deny the other team space in which to play.

Small-sided games emphasise the need for players to improve their individual skills, which enables teams to keep possession of the ball, creating more scoring opportunities. Soccer is more fun when individuals and teams have developed the skills needed to keep possession of the ball and score goals.

The following points for coaches will help the person in charge ensure that the games are successful and effective.

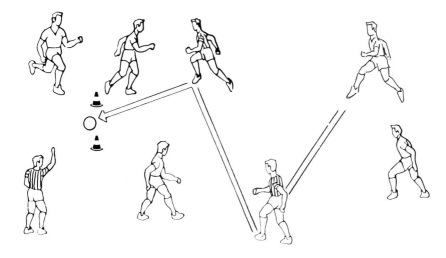

S M A L L - S I D E D   G A M E S

1. Allow players time to understand the basic idea of the game before introducing any variations.

2. Whenever possible, do not have more than six players in each team.

3. If there is an uneven amount of players, allow the extra player to play one half in one team and the second half in the other team.

4. If you have a large number of players, it is better to play two small-sided games where the players get plenty of touches rather than involve all the players in one large game.

5. If you introduce a variation and find it is not working, revert back to the basic idea of the game.

6. Encourage goalkeepers to throw the ball out, under head height, accurately.

7. Never let a game go on for too long. Keep a look out for signs of tiredness or lack of concentration.

8. Make sure the players use all the playing area.

9. Encourage players to call for the ball.

10. The most important point of all is to praise and encourage the players.

Practices

SMALL-SIDED GAMES

NUMBER OF PLAYERS

12 or more.

EQUIPMENT

Markers, bibs and a ball.

PLAYING AREA

60 metres by 40 metres.

THE PRACTICE

Divide the playing area into thirds, and at each end mark out two goals. Place the goalkeepers in the goals, and position the same amount of outfield players from each team in each third. These players must stay in their own area. The object of the practice is for each team, by passing and dribbling, to try and score goals. If the ball goes out of the playing area, it is rolled back in by the team whose possession it now is.

VARIATIONS

● Allow the middle players to go anywhere in the playing area.

● Allow the player who has passed the ball forward to follow it into that area.

● Restrict the players in the middle third to having only two touches, one to control and the other to pass.

● Goalkeepers are only allowed to serve the ball to players in their third.

SMALL-SIDED GAMES

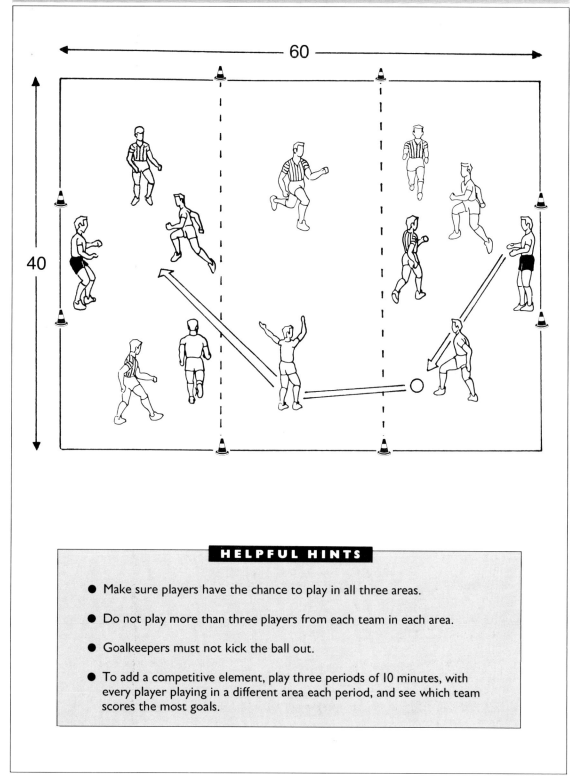

HELPFUL HINTS

- Make sure players have the chance to play in all three areas.

- Do not play more than three players from each team in each area.

- Goalkeepers must not kick the ball out.

- To add a competitive element, play three periods of 10 minutes, with every player playing in a different area each period, and see which team scores the most goals.

SMALL-SIDED GAMES

NUMBER OF PLAYERS

8 or more.

EQUIPMENT

Markers, bibs and a ball.

PLAYING AREA

50 metres by 30 metres.

THE PRACTICE

Divide the players into two teams and place the goalkeepers in the goals. The object of the practice is for both teams to score a goal. Before a shot can be taken, however, the player in possession must pass to a team-mate, who returns it using only one touch. The one-two only has to be played directly before a shot is taken – players can otherwise play freely, trying to find a shooting opportunity. If the ball goes out of the playing area it is rolled back in by the team whose possession it now is.

VARIATIONS

- Ask players to make a first-time shot after playing a one-two.

- Designate one player from each team with whom team-mates must play a one-two before taking a shot.

- Award a goal to either of the teams if they can make five consecutive one-touch passes.

- All passes and shots must be played along the ground.

S M A L L - S I D E D   G A M E S

- For younger players, start the practice with 'free' soccer before making them play one-twos to shoot.

- Also with younger players, allow the player receiving the first pass in the one-two to have a controlling touch.

- This is a difficult practice and many passes will go astray, but keep encouraging players to try.

- To add a competitive edge, award a goal for a successful one-two which finishes with a shot.

SMALL-SIDED GAMES

NUMBER OF PLAYERS
10 or more.

EQUIPMENT
One ball, markers and bibs.

PLAYING AREA
40 metres by 40 metres.

THE PRACTICE
Place a goalkeeper in the goal and position three defending players across a line, 20 metres out from the goal line. The rest of the players are organised into teams of five and are positioned at the opposite end of the playing area. The object of the practice is for the five attacking players who are in possession of the ball to try to score a goal. The three defending players, by tackling or intercepting passes, try to stop them. If they or the goalkeeper win possession of the ball they pass it back to the starting point, where the next five players are ready to go. If the ball goes out of the playing area, that again is the end of the attack and the attacking players move quickly out of the playing area to allow the next five players to start. The practice continues with the same three defenders staying in the playing area for a set period of time.

VARIATIONS

- Allow the defenders to use the offside rule.

- Only allow the attacking players to shoot after they have made four or more passes.

- Add a fourth defender.

- Only allow players to score with a header or a volley.

- Play five defenders, one as a sweeper, and add another attacker.

HELPFUL HINTS

- Make sure the defenders always start at the same point, 20 metres out from the goal-line.

- All aspects of attacking and defensive play can be practised in this game.

- Only practise one aspect at a time in each session. For example, how the attacking players can get more shots, or how the three defenders can defend against five attackers.

- Add a competitive edge by seeing which five attackers score most goals, and which three defenders let in least goals.

S M A L L - S I D E D   G A M E S

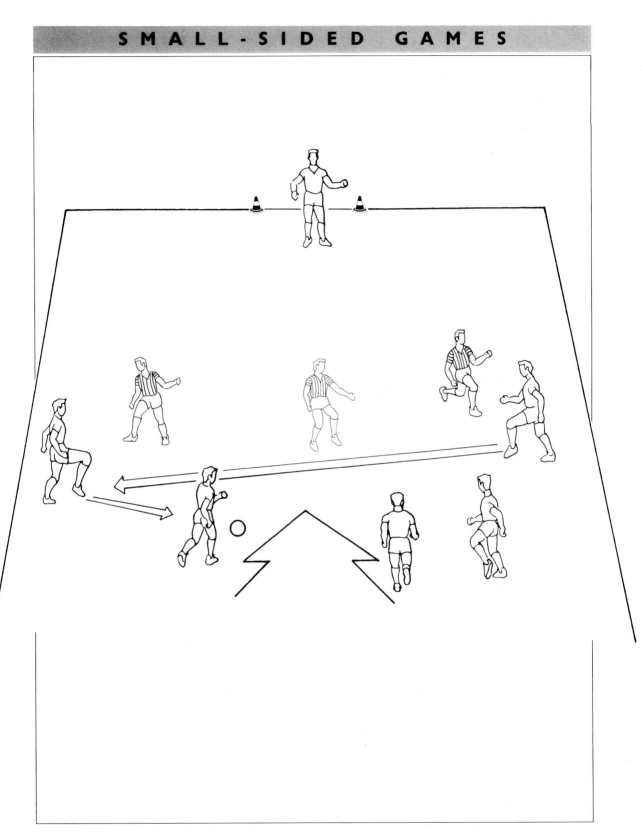

S M A L L - S I D E D   G A M E S

NUMBER OF PLAYERS
8 or more.

EQUIPMENT
One ball, markers and bibs.

PLAYING AREA
50 metres by 30 metres.

THE PRACTICE
Divide the players into two teams. Within the playing area, mark out 1-metre wide goals in any one of the three positions shown in the diagram opposite. The object of each of these practices is to pass the ball through either of the goals, from either side, to score. When a goal is scored the game is restarted, with a player in the team which has conceded the goal passing the ball out from that goal line. Play with the goals set out in one position for a period of time before changing to either of the other two.

VARIATIONS

- Increase the width of the goals.

- Number the goals and only allow the teams to score in designated goals.

- Players must dribble the ball through the goal to score.

- Nominate one player from each team to play freely, whilst the rest of the team are only allowed two touches, one to control, the next to pass.

- Only allow players to score through the front of the goals.

HELPFUL HINTS

- Do not allow defending players to stand between the markers.

- If you wish to include goalkeepers, make the goals they are positioned in full size.

- For younger players, decrease the distance between the goals.

- Make the practice competitive by seeing which team scores the most goals in 15 minutes.

S M A L L - S I D E D   G A M E S

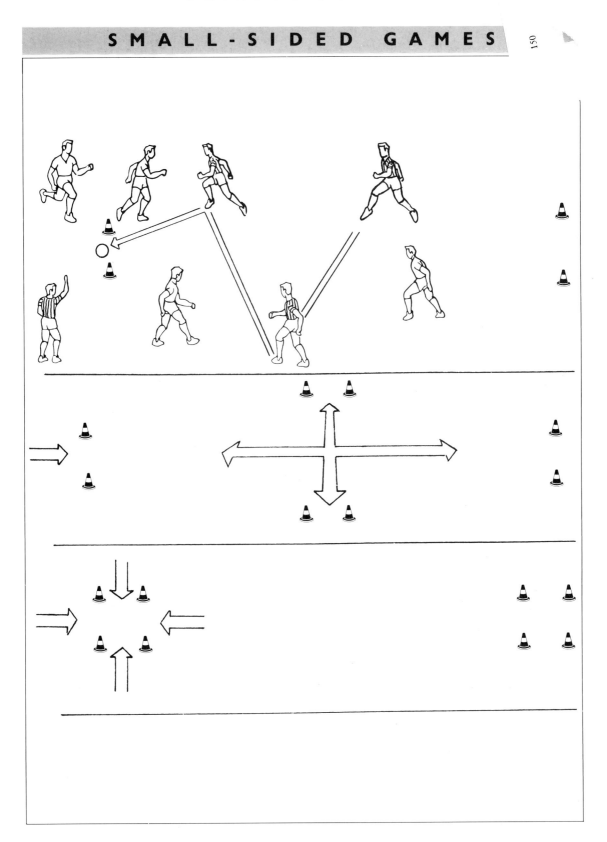

SMALL-SIDED GAMES

NUMBER OF PLAYERS

10 or more.

EQUIPMENT

Markers, bibs and a ball.

PLAYING AREA

40 metres by 40 metres.

THE PRACTICE

Place the goalkeepers in the goals. All but two of the rest of the players are divided into just two teams. These two remaining players are positioned just outside the touchlines and play with whichever team is in possession of the ball. Either of these two wide players must be involved in every attack but cannot score. They must stay outside the playing area but are allowed to move with or without the ball along the full length of the touchline. After a goal is scored, or the ball is retrieved from behind the goal, the goalkeeper restarts the practice, but is not allowed to pass directly to the two wide players. When the ball goes over the touchline the wide players re-start the game.

VARIATIONS

● Only allow players to score if they have received a direct pass from an outside player.

● Only allow a goal to be scored if both outside players have touched the ball in an attack.

● Only allow the two outside players two touches, one to control and the next to pass.

● Goalkeepers must throw the ball directly out to the wide players.

SMALL-SIDED GAMES

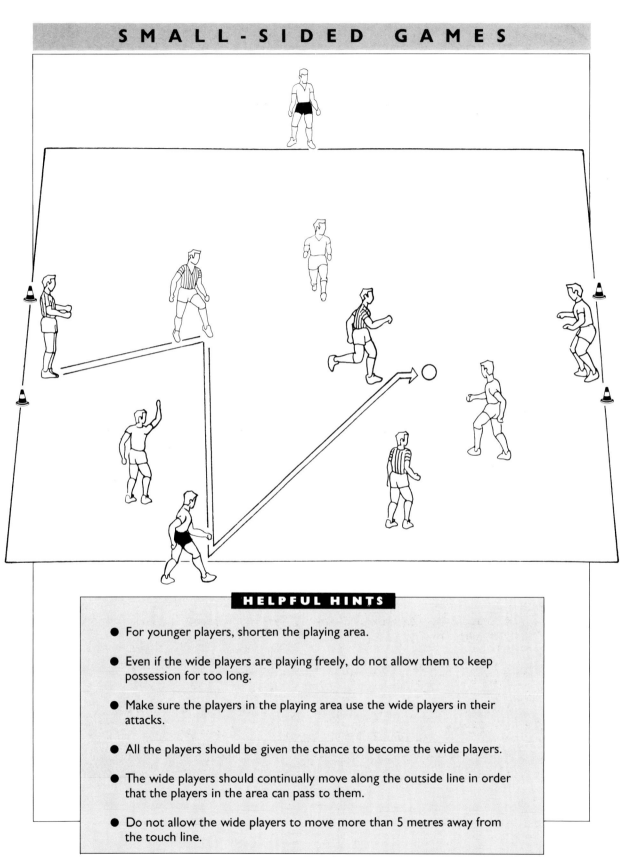

HELPFUL HINTS

● For younger players, shorten the playing area.

● Even if the wide players are playing freely, do not allow them to keep possession for too long.

● Make sure the players in the playing area use the wide players in their attacks.

● All the players should be given the chance to become the wide players.

● The wide players should continually move along the outside line in order that the players in the area can pass to them.

● Do not allow the wide players to move more than 5 metres away from the touch line.

S M A L L - S I D E D   G A M E S

NUMBER OF PLAYERS

6 or more.

EQUIPMENT

One ball and a net.

PLAYING AREA

20 metres by 10 metres.

THE PRACTICE

Mark out a 20 metre by 10 metre area and position a 2-metre high net across the middle of the playing area. Divide the players into two equal teams and position the teams each side of the net. The object of the game is for each team to keep the ball off the ground and to pass it over the net to land inside the opposing team's playing area. Each player can have as many touches as they like before passing to another member of their team or playing it over the net. If the ball fails to go over the net or goes out of the playing area, the team who last touched the ball loses possession. Services are made from the back of the playing area and points can only be won by the serving team.

VARIATIONS

- Restrict the players to two touches before the ball goes back over the net

- Only allow the players one touch.

- Ask all the players in the team to have a touch before the ball goes back over the net.

- Ask the players to play the ball back over the net using only their feet.

- Only allow the players to head the ball over the net.

- Allow the players to let the ball bounce once on their side of the net before playing it.

SMALL-SIDED GAMES

HELPFUL HINTS

● Position the players in each team to cover the whole of their playing area and make sure they take turns to play in all parts of the area.

● If a net isn't available, use markers, benches, or anything to separate the two areas.

● Make sure each player takes a turn to serve.

● Add a competitive edge by seeing which team scores 10 points first.

SMALL-SIDED GAMES

NUMBER OF PLAYERS
8 or more.

EQUIPMENT
Markers, bibs and a ball.

PLAYING AREA
50 metres by 30 metres.

THE PRACTICE
Divide the players into two teams and place the goalkeepers in the goals. Each player is given an opposing player to mark. The player in possession of the ball can only be tackled by their designated marking player, but every player is allowed to intercept passes. If the ball goes out of play, or a corner is awarded, the ball is rolled back in by the team whose possession it now is.

VARIATIONS

- Ask the teams to have three consecutive passes before taking a shot.

- Make players have at least three touches before they pass or shoot.

- Allow the players in one pair to tackle any of the opposing players.

- Play without goalkeepers, and make the goals two metres wide.

S M A L L - S I D E D   G A M E S

HELPFUL HINTS

- Goalkeepers should roll the ball accurately to a player in their team.

- Younger players should be paired with somebody of their own size and ability.

- Make sure players do not hold the player they are marking to gain an advantage.

- Encourage players to move sharply, to try to lose their markers.

- If a player tackles any player other than their designated player, award a penalty against them.

- Give a fun punishment to the player whose designated opponent has just scored.

SMALL-SIDED GAMES

NUMBER OF PLAYERS

9 or more.

EQUIPMENT

Markers, bibs and one ball.

PLAYING AREA

40 metres by 20 metres.

THE PRACTICE

Organise the players into two teams. One team attempts to score in the full-size goal, the other into either of the two small goals which are positioned at the opposite end of the playing area and are 2 metres wide and 20 metres apart. Only the team shooting into the two smaller goals has a goalkeeper. When the ball goes out of play, it is rolled back in unless a corner is awarded. After a period of time the teams change ends but the goalkeeper stays in the full-size goal.

VARIATIONS

● Only allow the players two touches – one to control and the next to pass.

● Do not allow the ball to be passed above head height.

● Award a goal if one team makes five consecutive passes.

● Play with just one small goal opposite the full-size goal and award three goals if a team passes the ball through it.

SMALL-SIDED GAMES

HELPFUL HINTS

● Allow both teams to have equal time shooting into the full-size goal.

● Encourage the team shooting into the full-size goal to have lots of shots.

● Only allow the goalkeeper to roll the ball to the players in their team.

● Do not allow the players defending the small goals to use their hands.

● Play 10 minutes each way and see which team scores the most goals.

SMALL-SIDED GAMES

NUMBER OF PLAYERS

11 or more.

EQUIPMENT

Markers, bibs and a ball.

PLAYING AREA

50 metres by 30 metres.

THE PRACTICE

Divide the players into three teams and place the goalkeepers in the goals. Two of the teams play against each other, trying to score goals. The third team joins in to play with whichever team has possession of the ball but any goals scored by this team are awarded to the team they are playing with. If the ball goes out of the playing area, it is rolled back in by the team whose possession it is. When a goal is scored, the goalkeeper restarts the game by rolling the ball back in. The practice continues with each of the three teams taking their turn to be the 'third' team.

VARIATIONS

- Do not allow the players to pass the ball above head height.

- Do not allow the players in the third team to shoot.

- Do not allow the players to pass back to the goalkeeper.

- Allow teams to be awarded a goal if they make five consecutive passes.

- Only allow the third team's players one or two touches.

SMALL-SIDED GAMES

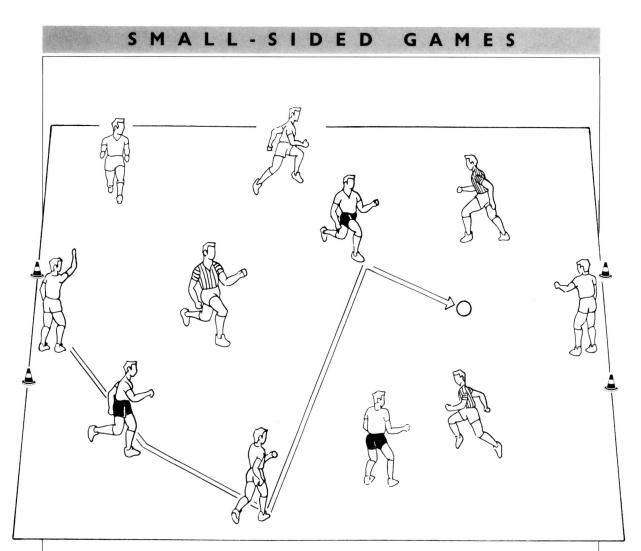

HELPFUL HINTS

● Encourage the players in possession of the ball to pass it quickly amongst themselves and use all of the playing area.

● The three defending players should work together, giving them more chance to win the ball.

● The team in possession of the ball should try to get as close to the goal as possible before shooting.

● To make the practice more competitive, play for three periods of 10 minutes and see which team concedes least goals.